CHASTITY

CHASTITY

Reconciliation of the Senses

ERIK VARDEN

BLOOMSBURY CONTINUUM
LONDON · OXFORD · NEW YORK · NEW DELHI · SYDNEY

BLOOMSBURY CONTINUUM
Bloomsbury Publishing Plc
50 Bedford Square, London, WC1B 3DP, UK
29 Earlsfort Terrace, Dublin 2, Ireland

BLOOMSBURY, BLOOMSBURY CONTINUUM and the Diana logo are
trademarks of Bloomsbury Publishing Plc

First published in Great Britain 2023

A catalogue record for this book is available from the British Library

Library of Congress Cataloguing-in-Publication data has been applied for

ISBN: TPB: 978-1-3994-1141-7; eBook: 978-1-3994-1140-0;
ePDF: 978-1-3994-1139-4

4 6 8 10 9 7 5 3

Typeset by Deanta Global Publishing Services, Chennai, India
Printed and bound in Great Britain by CPI Group (UK) Ltd, Croydon CR0 4YY

To find out more about our authors and books visit www.bloomsbury.com
and sign up for our newsletters

ubi amor, ibi oculus

Contents

List of Illustrations

Norma's Question

'Chastity' has become a word for antiquarians. It describes a set of attitudes and a code of behaviour associated with a past age. Many rejoice to see it bygone. Hearing the word spoken today, we are more likely to think of thwarted sexuality than of dew-besprinkled strength of virtue 'fresh as Dian's visage'.

The unravelling of sexual abuse committed by people, overwhelmingly men, who had professed a *vow* of chaste celibacy has rightly occasioned a surge of rage throughout society. The ideal of chastity appears discredited, certainly as a mandatory form of religious observance. Revealed to have been, often, not just lifeless but deadly, it is present to us now rather as a decomposing corpse awaiting burial. There is grief clinging to it, yes; but is there any reason to mourn its passing?

It is not my purpose to present an apology for chastity. Nor am I writing as a cultural historian intent on chronicling the demise of a human *habitus*. Mine is primarily a semantic concern.

I must point out, first, that chastity is not coterminous with celibacy. Celibacy is a particular, not particularly common, vocation. Chastity is a virtue for all. If the institutionalization of chastity has occasioned, or fed into, such frustration, such aberration, it is partly through a reduction of perspective whereby an orientation intended to broaden the heart has, instead, constrained it to the point of suffocation.

To tie chastity down, as has been done, to mere mortification of the senses is to make of it a tool to sabotage the flourishing of character. It is also to misunderstand, misrepresent and misapply the meaning of a complex notion. I hope, in this book, to release 'chastity' from imprisonment in too narrow categories, allowing it to stretch, extend its limbs, breathe freely, perhaps even sing. I use these images advisedly. Unless chastity has a degree of full-bloodedness, it is not the real thing, but counterfeit. I shall proceed partly by analysis, partly by examples. If I seem to cast my net disconcertingly wide, bear with me. It is as it must be, for we are, I hope you will come to agree, entering a field the length and breadth of which reach far, very far.

It would be disingenuous not to declare, from the outset, personal interest, even a personal agenda. I entered monastic life in 2002, at a time when cases of historical sexual abuse committed by clerics, including monks, were published so often, so fully, in the English press that I went through periods of continuous nausea. To receive the novice's habit in such a climate was strange. The garment that stood for my noblest, most joyful aspirations established me in some kind of symbolic continuity with the perpetration of deeds that had caused immense, in some cases irreparable, harm. It was hard not to feel contaminated by association and, to a greater or lesser extent, to interiorize a sense of guilt. This reflex was affirmed when, now and again, I caught a glimpse of what others might see when they saw me.

Let me explain what I mean.

A decade after my clothing, when the extent of sexual abuse in the Church was increasingly acknowledged all over Europe, I was making my way, one blue morning, towards the Roman basilica of Santa Maria Maggiore, bound for the Oriental Institute, where I was working. On the Via Panisperna, I encountered a middle-aged woman who with calm deliberation spat in my face. I could intuit the depth of wrath and hurt from which her action sprang. Perhaps I could even understand her. There was no way of finding out. She was in no mood to talk.

How might I respond?

That was, and remains, an urgent question for me. Just pious phrases will not do. The real answer must lie in my chaste commitment, in the integrity with which I live it out. For me, as someone who has taken public vows, chastity cannot be reduced to a private matter (though God knows it is that, too); I am held to account for it.

It does seem crucial, then, to have a clear, articulate understanding of exactly what chastity means. But how hard it can be to think and speak of chastity! How easily one comes to seem embarrassing, even to oneself!

There is a paradox here, given how unabashedly we speak of sex. I am of a generation for whom sex, following the cultural battles of the 1960s, had clatteringly descended from darkened bedrooms into the public square in what was intended to be a liberation. The mechanics of reproduction were taught in primary school alongside 'rithmetic and writing. Among teenage boys pornography was taken for granted – hardly in itself a cultural novelty, though its explicitness and copiousness were, leaving slowly healing wounds on the memory.

One was cautioned against the harmful effects of sexual inhibition. I am not suggesting we were indoctrinated. Still, the air one breathed in what I'd say was a pretty standard, Northern-European teenage environment in the 1980s was thick with sub-Freudian suppositions approximately understood, sometimes carelessly applied. These suppositions informed the interpretative paradigm readily to hand when, as an adolescent, I sought parameters by which to establish my place in the world, before the other, before God – in other words, a way to find freedom.

The accepted nomenclature for transcendence was psychosexual. Any yearning, any soul-pain was thought definable in its terms. The general assumption was that the pursuit of a well-balanced, complex-free sexual self was a prerequisite for growth, maturity and thriving.

It took me years to see that, in fact, the process works the other way round; that it does not make experiential sense to ascribe orientational autonomy to the sexual instinct, as if it were a naturally ordering force bound to align other aspects of one's being to itself in harmonious design. Human sexuality calls out for a structure of personhood upon which to grow, blossom and fruit, much the way a climbing rose needs trellises to rise and spread. Left to crawl on the ground, such a rose turns into a leafy heap. Its beauty will still be visible, by all means. Its fragrance will remain. But long stretches of stem will fail to bud for want of light. Its flowers will be few. Lacking strength to maintain upward momentum, it will collapse into itself. Any gardener's hand attempting to direct it once it has grown a while, once summer has come, will reach into a tangle of thorns.

In his Rule for monks, St Benedict describes a human type that corresponds to this horticultural metaphor. It is that of the *gyrovague*, a type of vagrant seeker who spends life walking round and round, without arriving at any determinate destination. The *gyrus*, in Latin, was the ring in which horses were trained, or the course of a mule that turned a well's waterwheel, a circuit of aimless drudgery. Such a *gyrovague* was I, for unnecessarily long, with regard to my maturing as a man.

Looking back, I feel a mixture of regret and wry amusement. For the well around which I dragged my feet was dry. It had never had a drop of water in it. Its morosely two-dimensional account of life and love was a heap of dry bones. Yet I kept circling it, bound to a yoke made up of projections, troubled by the thought that my awakening to faith, going on at the same time, might be nothing but unhealthy sublimation. Was it fear of nature that impelled me towards the supernatural?

Such can the strength of conjecture be that it seems more real than reality. I aspired to live chastely, but regarded the endeavour as sheer mortification. It did not occur to me, I think, to see chastity as possessing an intrinsic, never mind life-giving attraction. I thought of it in negative terms, as *not* being, *not* doing what lay at the heart of the contemporary image of masculinity. Hence a further complex arose. In a culture glorifying sexual expression, was chastity not somehow unmanly?

If only I had thought of reading Cicero!

He could have let me discover that, in the ancient world, the goddess of chastity, Diana, was known not only as *lucifera*, 'light-bearing', but as *omnivaga*, 'roaming everywhere', so sovereign and free – the antithesis of the *gyrovague.* These associations would have appealed to me and cheered me as I retraced my steps in a barren furrow.

For of course I desired openness and light. I desire them still.

What does 'chastity' mean? The word 'chaste' reached English through the Romance languages from the Latin *castus*, which in turn is traceable to the Greek adjective καθαρός (*katharos*), meaning 'pure'. From *katharos* we get *catharsis*. We might spend a moment considering the sense that word grew to fathom.

Aristotle, in his *Poetics*, uses *catharsis* as an image for inward cleansing that may come about in one who goes to see a tragic play. Observing the rendering on stage of strong, normally hidden emotion, being invested in the drama by an empathy at once intellectual and visceral, the viewer may tap these same depths in him or herself.

Thus a potentially remarkable process is enabled to begin. The purpose of tragic performance, says Aristotle, is to effect the representation – or, to use his term, the *mimesis* – of universal human affairs; not to invent outlandish plots for the purpose of engendering a thrill, but to spell out scenarios in which spectators may recognize themselves to get in touch with their inner reserves.

These reserves can be positively or negatively coloured. Aristotle speaks, by way of example, of pity and fear, responses that stand for a wide gamut of 'passions' [παθήματα]. *Com*passion with the enacted drama brings hidden depths into conscious awareness, relieving a charge that, left pent-up, conditions our behaviour and thought in ways that escape the mind's conscious attention and so curtail our freedom, the way we make choices.

To feel grief for the predicament of Phaedra, whose heart is torn apart by an impossible love; to find, watching Ingrid Bergman's *Autumn Sonata*, that one's stomach churns with the rage of Eva claiming her voice after a lifetime's submission to maternal tyranny dressed up as care: this is not to indulge in auto-suggestion but to expose oneself willingly to extreme experience, prepared to recognize its resonance, however faint, in oneself, so to permit what, in the depths of self, may have been implicit or suppressed to find outward form, with an inward sigh of relief.

That Aristotle names this process 'purification' cautions us against defining 'purity' in cultic terms, as if standing in straightforward opposition to the intrinsically 'impure'; it speaks rather of an equilibrium regained by means of engagement with passions which run wild, to bring these back like rebellious horses under reason's sway. Aristotle's pedagogy has perennial value.

The semantic range of *katharos* spilt over into '*castus*', its Latin equivalent. Lewis and Short, in their *Latin Dictionary*, equate *castus* with *integer*, noting that the term was generally used 'in respect to the person himself', not so much 'in respect to other men'. Chastity, in other words, is a marker of integrity, of a personality whose parts are assembled in harmonious completeness.

There are telling examples of usage. Listing, in his treatise *On Divination*, means by which the gods make their ways known to men, Cicero says it is all very well to read the constellations of the stars or the flight of birds, then to try to understand them; but that a man is unlikely to grasp the signified meaning of phenomena unless his soul ('*animus*') is 'chaste and pure' ('*castus purusque*'). By this, he intends lucid open-spiritedness, a freedom from passionate bias, quite as in the instance of Aristotle's theatregoer at the end of an effective performance.

This epistemological dimension of 'chastity' is taken further in the *First Tusculan Disputation*. Citing Socrates, Cicero outlines the two ways in which human beings may leave this life. Those blinded by vice – the debauched or profligate, the selfish politicians – will have erred from the goodness and beauty of the gods and be unfit to enjoy their fellowship forever. Such people, he says, have cause to dread death's hour. Those, meanwhile, who have kept themselves chaste and entire (*'qui se integros castosque servavissent'*), not reducing existence to self-indulgence but keeping their minds in ascent, may look forward to beatitude hereafter.

To be chaste in this life is to attune oneself to celestial life, and so have reason to die, says Cicero, 'like a swan, with singing and desire'.

Aulus Gellius, the second-century grammarian, applied chastity to literary style. Like his colleagues in every age, Gellius thought he was living in a time of linguistic decadence. He invoked the register of 'chastity' to praise the prose of Caesar. It stood, he thought, for a standard the world might never know again, for Caesar was *'sermonis praeter alios suae aetatis castissimi'* ('of a purity of speech exceeding that of his contemporaries'), in a position to address put-downs even to Cicero, whom Caesar found to be employing unnecessary loan-words.

To be *un*chaste, it is implied, is to corrupt the elegance of a coherent whole by introducing elements not connatural to it.

From this semantic base, *'castus'* found its way into the terminology of sexual morality, whether to describe an object ('a chaste marriage bed'), a person ('a chaste matron'), or a physical feature ('a chaste countenance'). These notions are far from the mindset suggested by the medieval 'chastity belt', a metal cast with lock and key designed to place the sexual organs out of bounds, whether such a contraption was ever used or merely reflects the prurient fantasy of later times.

For one thing, chastity is not a denial of sex. It is an orientation of sexuality, of the whole vital instinct, towards a desired finality. It is a function of wholeness sought and healing found.

The examples I have adduced display an intellectual dimension. It matters to one who would be *castus* (or *casta*) to have a clear idea of motivating purpose.

This concern is evidenced, too, in the cluster of words which came to represent 'chastity' in the Germanic languages, although these sprang from quite another root. Contemporary forms such as *keusch*, *kuis* or *kysk* have their origin in a Gothic term, *kūskeis*, derived from the Latin *conscius*. In this lexical family, 'chastity' supposes, first, a *conscious* awareness of the good, whole and pure; then, a will to construct one's life by these values.

In my mother tongue, Norwegian, the modern derivative adjective, *kysk*, has long since been consigned to vocabulary's dustbin. Recycling was not an option. The word had acquired a sense so rigid and frigid that in the end it was useless even for purposes of satire. It simply made one cringe.

This provides food for thought. A term that, at heart, signifies the *conscious* education of the sexual drive (as physical passion, as capacity for tenderness, as will to live fully), envisaging the gradual attuning of body, mind and soul, had degenerated into a marker of cold *dis*incarnation. Lost was a vision of 'chastity' supposing, not the suppression or oppression of sex, but its maturing, with a view to flourishing and fruitfulness. In a Christian

optic, one would have to add: and with a view to *glory*.
For the Christian life is life oriented towards beatitude.

How did this impoverishment happen?

Tantalizing clues may be found in what must be
the Western world's most famous hymn to chastity, a
contender for countless people's *Desert Island Discs*. The
aria *Casta Diva* from Vicenzo Bellini's opera *Norma* is
inseparable from the legacy of Maria Callas, who made
of it her signature piece, singing it throughout her career
with the *bravura* that behoved her status as a 'diva' in
the commoner sense. Francis Poulenc, who heard her in
Milan, was at once appalled and enchanted to see how, at
curtain call, she dextrously shoved her tenor co-star 'into
the corner of the wings and advanced by herself into the
middle of the stage' to be adored by her audience. The
association of *Casta Diva* with grand theatricality, vocal
pyrotechnics and rapturous applause may have caused us
to pay scant attention to the text. So here it is:

> *Casta diva, che inargenti*
> *Queste sacre antiche piante,*
> *A noi volgi il bel sembiante,*
> *Senza nube e senza vel!*
> *Tempra, o Diva,*
> *Tempra tu de' cori ardenti,*
> *Tempra ancora lo zelo audace.*
> *Spargi in terra quella pace*
> *Che regnar tu fai nel ciel.*

> Chaste Goddess, giver of a silver sheen
> to these ancient, sacred trees,
> turn your lovely countenance
> unclouded, unveiled towards us.

Temper, Goddess,
temper still the bold zeal
of impassioned hearts.
Scatter on earth that same peace
which you cause to reign in heaven

On the face of it, this seems pretty harmless and harmlessly pretty: a myrtle-crowned maiden in flowing robes imploring the moon, Diana's emblem, to shed her chaste light on a troubled world and to grant peace to souls.

In reality, the scene is highly ambiguous. The drama of *Norma* is enacted in Gaul roughly at the time of chastely-speaking Caesar's conquest. The heroine is a priestess of Irminsul, a Germanic divinity whose idol, a stripped oak, has roots that reach back to the cosmic tree of Norse mythology, Ygdrasil, possessed of sinuous branches embracing earth, heaven and hell.

Formally speaking, Norma embodies chastity: on acceding to her office she had taken a vow of virginity. She is tied to the altar, says she towards the end of Act One, with an 'eternal knot'. But she has not been faithful.

Having fallen in love with the Roman Proconsul Pollione, her people's chief enemy, Norma had borne him two sons in stealth. She secretly remains in thrall to his affection. She will do anything to maintain it. The peace she invokes upon Gaul in this aria is no disinterested peace. It is a ruse by which she hopes to protect her lover from her kin, athirst for Roman blood. For years she has presented as inspired oracles what is simply the dictate of her heart: that no sword be brandished against Pollione. Her hope is that the Proconsul will take her and her children to Rome. The warbling maiden, then, is a perjurer and an impostor.

The soprano Giuditta Pasta, Bellini's first Norma, in her costume, looking like a First-Communicant directing guests towards the buffet, though sinisterly flanked by the stump of Irminsul.

She is also a tormented, desperately unhappy soul. Norma does not trust Pollione to be constant. Immediately after singing *Casta Diva*, she turns aside and addresses a secret prayer, no longer to the moon, but to the father of her children:

Ah! bello a me ritorna
Del fido amor primiero,
E contro il mondo intiero
Difesa a te sarò.

Oh, beautiful man, return to me
something of our first, faithful love,
and I, against the whole world,
shall be your defence.

There is stuff here for pathos, for Norma's hunch is right:
Pollione has quite lost interest in her. He is now in love
with her novice Adalgisa, whom he intends to abduct
and marry, leaving Norma to the dismal darkness of
Irminsul's grove.

This is not all. Bellini's librettist, Felice Romani, based
his text on a tragedy by the French playwright Alexandre
Soumet (1788–1845). Soumet, not much read now, was in
his day a towering figure, a member of the French Academy
and a pioneer in the composition of new patriotic epics
needed in a time of violent disruptions, when history was
constantly rewritten in the light of the currently reigning
world view. *Norma, ou l'Infanticide*, first performed
in 1831, was the sixth in a series of feminine portraits
that extended from Clytemnestra to Jeanne d'Arc. The
character Norma was Soumet's free invention, though he
borrowed traits from earlier works. His play is an example
of post-revolutionary France's interest in the Celtic past,
an interest tending to be vague in its references, liberal in
its syntheses.

Soumet spells out a part of Norma's story that Bellini
and Romani leave implicit. We learn that she had, as a
young woman, been held hostage in Rome and had

come, in fact, to regard herself as Roman. Privately she calls the city 'my second fatherland', yet repatriation and ordination as priestess had forced her to adopt, in public, an anti-Roman stance. In the opera, Norma's divided loyalties find supreme expression precisely in *Casta Diva*. Diana, saluted in the figure of the moon, had no place within the Gallic pantheon. True, Bellini lets Norma's father, Oroveso, and the chorus repeat her invocation, but that is pure artistic licence on his part. Really, Norma's prayer to a Roman goddess is apostasy to Irminsul and, to boot, a betrayal of her people's national cult, the heart and soul of their struggle for autonomy.

The scene is thus charged with the irony of multiply accumulated *un*chastities: the apparently celibate Norma is on fire with illicit love; her children are concealed in the shrine of the god to whom she had trothed virginity; invoking the goddess of the Romans she betrays at once her nation and her faith, revealing a heart in conflict with her public persona; her prayer for the tempering of zeal is in fact a prelude to her knowing abandonment of reason, to issue in bloodthirsty rage. Her prayer to the 'chaste goddess' is marked by hopelessness. Norma seemingly takes it for granted that the human heart is fickle, and doomed to stay thus, so that any committal of it, whether to an earthly or to a transcendent love, must be temporary.

The drama of *Norma* contains a single Christian character: Norma's children's nurse Clotilde. Will she, who believes in an incarnate God and in humanity's capacity for divinization, offer helpful counsel, a sense of direction, perhaps? No.

In the opera Clotilde is reduced to a faintly comical walk-on part devoid of consequence. In the play she is more amply drawn. Her faith, though, has little to say for itself. It is too otherworldly: before God, she proclaims, the universe is as nothing, 'like a bird in the hollow of your hand'. Clotilde's Christian profession is bland. When Norma asks a question deserving a serious answer, 'Does your God *heal* hearts sick with love?', Clotilde answers with a sigh, 'He appeases them.'

Appeasement! Is that all Christianity has to offer a wounded heart crying out to love and be loved, to know and be known? Must the Christian just wait and burn while fire within spends itself and live coals turn into ashes? Has he or she no other response to love's passion than resignation, eyes mournfully raised heavenward?

Often it has seemed thus. It is a blessing that the cultural shift of recent decades has exposed how harmful a rhetoric of appeasement, drenched in piety, can be when used to silence the voracious hunger of the human heart. Instead of bringing healing, anaesthetics of devout abstraction are prone to *cause* sickness in the form of arrested tenderness, of vulnerability soured into spite, of unmet affective need seeking satisfaction in addiction or cruelty, or in gradual petrification.

If appeasement is all she is offered in lieu of a cure, it would seem that Norma is *destined* to sing her anguished heart out, as at the beginning of Bellini's opera, then to throw herself off the edge of a cliff, as at the end of Soumet's play.

Clotilde's capitulation is representative, alas, of much Christian discourse of the past few hundred years. This discourse has much to answer for. In the pages that follow, I will try to broaden a scope that has been scandalously narrowed, redrawing a Christian understanding of chastity based on the classical heritage we have considered, but reaching further. A Christian view of chastity, if it is genuine, is not simplistic. It determinedly embraces the complex fullness of our human condition no less than the divine fulfilment to which that nature is called.

The Christian view of what it is to be sexual, and so, by extension, what it is to be chaste, presupposes a particular view of what it is to be human. My next chapter restates a view of human nature drawn from Scripture, in particular from the first three chapters of Genesis. The early Christians read this *protology*, the account of the world's beginning, with attention. The text speaks of man's making in the image and likeness of God. Some of the Fathers imagined this likeness as a robe of glory. The nakedness that suddenly bewildered Adam and Eve after the fall stood for the loss of this robe, for which the *protoplasts*, our first parents, tried to make amends by covering themselves with matter. The proverbial fig leaves, however, were strictly pro tem. At the end of Genesis 3, we are told that God, before expelling them from paradise, 'made for Adam and for his wife garments of skins, and clothed them' (Genesis 3.21). This is theology in images. In the sequence of clothing, undressing and reclothing, the Fathers found a hermeneutic key to human experience. We may profitably try that key in some of our own rusted padlocks.

My central chapter considers the challenge of maturing to chastity through the prism of multiple tensions. Few find their way to integrity without a sense of being pulled in different directions. The experience may recur at different times of life in different ways. There can be joy in it. There can also be a sense of agonizing conflict. Who has not, at one time or another, stood aghast in front of the bathroom mirror forced to admit what Paul bravely confessed to the Romans, 'I do not understand my own actions' (Rom. 7.15)? We are often a riddle to ourselves.

Interior contradiction is treated squarely in Christian tradition, which helps us identify the balancing acts of which our lives consist. Chastity stands for equilibrium. It stands, too, for fearlessness as we find that our homecoming to ourselves, which is what becoming chaste amounts to, is not so much an anxious manoeuvring between Scylla and Charybdis, menaces about us, as the progressive integration of possibilities within. Constantine Cavafy, in his splendid poem 'Ithaca', affirms that the goal of our life's odyssey is found *in* the journey, in a reconciled fullness that embraces both spirit and flesh:

Τοὺς Λαιστρυγόνας καὶ τοὺς Κύκλωπας,
τὸν θυμωμένο Ποσειδῶνα μὴ φοβᾶσαι,
τέτοια στὸν δρόμο σου ποτέ σου δὲν θὰ βρεῖς,
ἂν μέν' ἡ σκέψις σου ὑψηλή, ἂν ἐκλεκτὴ
συγκίνησις τὸ πνεῦμα καὶ τὸ σῶμα σου ἀγγίζει.

Τοὺς Λαιστρυγόνας καὶ τοὺς Κύκλωπας,
τὸν ἄγριο Ποσειδώνα δὲν θὰ συναντήσεις,
ἂν δὲν τοὺς κουβανεῖς μὲς στὴν ψυχή σου,
ἂν ἡ ψυχή σου δὲν τοὺς στήνει ἐμπρός σου.

Do not fear the Cyclops,
Laestrygonians, or angry Poseidon.
Such you will never find along your way
If your thoughts stay high, if choice emotions
Touch your body and your spirit.

You will never meet the Cyclops,
Laestrygonians, or angry Poseidon
Unless you carry them inside your soul,
Unless your soul props them up before you.

My fourth chapter looks at the negotiation of passions from a monastic point of view. Why bother? Because monasticism was, from earliest times, a theological laboratory. While councils, ecumenical and partisan, argued and fought over points of doctrine, the Church's faith was put to the test in a parallel, experiential universe: that of the monasteries. The early monks and nuns were seekers after coherence. They wished to live in a way that realized their potential as men and women created in the image of the Word made flesh. This included the pursuit of chaste integrity. Endowed with self-knowledge, unafraid to call a spade a spade, these brothers and sisters of ours, though they lived long ago, provide insight to illumine and assist us still, floundering as we are in our post-postmodernity.

This chapter on the monastic quest culminates in an exposition of different ways of seeing. In fact, you will find that the motif of sight runs like a thread throughout the book. To inhabit the world chastely is to see it in truth and to see myself and humankind truthfully within it – that is, to become a contemplative. Contemplative life is often envisaged as near-disembodied, an existence of angelic aspiration or presumption. This is a ridiculous notion. The human being as such is contemplative. I submit that much perplexity regarding our nature springs from failure to acknowledge this dimension of who we are, all of us. That is why I have written, as a coda, a final chapter on contemplation, thinking it might usefully cast light from a different angle on the argument preceding it.

I began this introduction with a disclaimer. I must conclude with another: I make no claim to completeness. The present book is not a treatise. It is an essay.

Some readers will be annoyed that little is said in celebration of sexuality enacted as a nuptial dimension of our divinely imaged nature. This is a noble theme, embedded in Scripture. One has but to think of the Song of Songs, which a strand of rabbinic tradition considered the holiest book in the canon. If I have refrained from engaging more explicitly with this theme, it is on account of my state of life. I write as a man engaged to live celibately; this colours my own understanding of chastity. It enriches and limits my perspective. In a matter such as this, one must speak of what one *knows*. I invite others to make contributions from other vantage points. More are needed, from men and women. If my inadequacies inspire others to pursue their own Christian reflection on this theme, I shall be delighted.

Other readers, knowing the book's author to be a Roman Catholic bishop, will be peeved that little is said about controversial issues in explicit defence of the Church's moral doctrine. I am committed to this doctrine. I believe in its goodness and reasonableness. Anyone who wishes to know what the Catholic Church does teach on a given subject can open that great treasure trove, the 1992 *Catechism*, which raised this genre of literature to a new level. I spend much of my time expounding this teaching and making it known: that's my job, quite simply.

This book's purpose is different, however – which is not to say it is unrelated to my episcopal charge. A bishop's ministry is 'pontifical'. To be a *pontifex* is to build bridges. Given the amnesia to which the West has succumbed regarding its Christian patrimony, a chasm extends between 'secular' society and the Church's sacred shore. When attempts are made to holler across, we risk misunderstanding: for even when the same words are used on either side, they have acquired different meanings. What poses as 'dialogue' easily ends up being a *dialogue de sourds*. Bridges are needed to enable encounter. Christians must present their faith integrally, without temporizing compromise; at the same time, they must express it in ways comprehensible to those ill-informed about formal dogma. They will often do this most effectively by appealing to universal experience, then trying to read such experience in the light of revelation.

That is how the Fathers preached. That is why their words ring still with such engaging clarity. We must learn to speak likewise, grateful for the riches passed down from of old and respectful, at the same time, of our own strange times. No life-giving word was ever uttered with scorn.

In Jerome's rendering of the First Epistle of Peter, the Apostle exhorts us: '*Animas vestras castificantes in oboedientia charitatis in fraternitatis amore simplici ex corde invicem diligite attentius*'. We could put this into English as follows: 'Making your souls chaste in the obedience of charity, in love of the brotherhood, having become whole, love one another from the heart more attentively' (1.22). It is a bracing statement. St Peter teaches that attentive love requires, on the part of the loving subject, wholeness born of a chaste endeavour conceived of in terms of a transitive, dynamic verb – '*castificantes*' – not of a lazy noun that spells the effect of passive, appeased resignation.

The essence of becoming chaste is not a putting-to-death of our nature, but its orientation, enacted through integral reconciliation, towards fullness of life.

What a Human Being *Is*

The Roman rite of the liturgy of Mass preserves, at the offertory, a telling ritual. It occurs just after the priest has received the host from the acolyte and placed it on the corporal, named for its function of holding the Lord's Body, *Corpus Domini*: a square piece of linen symbolizing at once the Infant's swaddling clothes and the Crucified's shroud, a sign that God encounters, carries and saves us bodily. The acolyte next brings the chalice into which the priest pours, first wine, then a tiny drop of water. Wine is richly significant in Jewish-Christian tradition. In the context of the eucharistic liturgy, we recognize in it a representation of Christ's divinity. The water, meanwhile, stands for our humanity.

The disproportion between the elements is not just quantitive, it is metaphysical. 'The mystery of faith!' the priest will exclaim a little later. Here we are at the heart of it. In the incarnation, mystically exhibited on the altar, the uncreated being of God is united to our contingent nature. The union is immediate and perfect. In the chalice, the water does not stay a discernible entity apart, the way oil would have done. It merges with the wine. It even brings out a new quality in it, revealing a fresh potential: think of how a connoisseur drops water into young claret to boost oxidization and release flavour. While performing this action, the priest recites the following, very ancient prayer:

Deus qui humanae substantiae dignitatem mirabiliter condidisti et mirabilius reformasti: da nobis, per huius aquae et vini mysterium, eius divinitatis esse consortes, qui humanitatis nostrae fieri dignatus est particeps.

God, who wonderfully formed the dignity of human substance, then reformed it even more wonderfully; grant us by this mystery of water and wine to be sharers in his divinity, who deigned to partake of our humanity.

The act of creation is evoked by the choice of a tactile verb, *condere*. To get a sense of it, recall that, in German, it developed into '*Konditor*', a pastry chef, who brings forth delicious creations through careful handling. Origen had this aspect of creation in mind when he observed that the Lord, having made each other part of the universe by means of a word – 'God said . . . and there was' – on the sixth day made man, uniquely, with his hands: 'The Lord God formed man of dust from the ground, and breathed into his nostrils the breath of life; and man became a living being' (Genesis 2.7).

The offertory prayer speaks of God's act of forming 'the dignity of human substance'. The phrase 'human substance' sounds clunky. It is not one we would ordinarily use, but here we must if we are not to miss the point: the very *matter* of humanity is wonderfully fashioned and dignified. Our initial form was wonderful. It was then deformed. But God wrought a re-formation that rendered it more wonderful still, apt, by grace, to commune in divine nature.

With consummate economy, this prayer, recited daily worldwide at countless altars on behalf of all humanity, puts the origin and finality of our nature before us. An account of chaste living must unfold within this perspective, attentive not just to what and where we are now, but to where we come from, to where we are going.

CREATED 'IN THE IMAGE'

The verse, 'Let us make man in our image, after our likeness' (Genesis 1.26), is probably the most exegeted passage of Scripture. Sages both Jewish and Christian have pored over it for millennia, dissecting every syllable, letter and diacritical sign. Yet even a fleeting acquaintance with the Old Testament reveals that God *has* no image. The mere thought of fashioning such a thing is considered an enormity.

How, then, can God be said to communicate it? How can the human being embody it? Evidently God did not envisage man as a walking idol. Jonathan Sacks, whose voice I sorely miss, remarked that the word 'image' must refer to something

quite different from the possession of a specific form. The fundamental point of Genesis 1 is that God transcends nature. Therefore, He is free, unbounded by nature's laws. By creating human beings 'in his image', God gave us a similar freedom, thus creating the one being capable itself of being creative.

This is true. Yet the Fathers saw a further, ontological dimension in this formula. They found in it a statement of what human beings have it in them to become.

They were careful not to read Genesis anthropomorphically. They were wary of fancying God, as it were, at work before a mirror, casting glances at his reflection, then reproducing what he saw in clay intended to become a material self-portrait. Rather, our ancestors in faith fed the phrase 'in our image' into their inward concordance, available to them since they knew much of Scripture by heart. They were keen to make Biblical sense of what the word 'image' might really stand for.

So they found the creation account illumined and explained by a statement occurring near the end of the canon, when St Paul, imprisoned, tells the Church in Colossae of its call to 'share in the inheritance of the saints in light'. Christians, says Paul, must know they have been raised out of darkness by the Father's only Son who *is* 'the image of the invisible God' (1.12-15). The 'image' at once ceases to be an abstraction. It comes to designate a presence. For man to be made 'in the image' is for him to subsist, by nature, 'in the Son'. The human form is seen from the outset to point towards the Son's incarnation.

Only the embodiment in person of God's *eikōn* will perfect human nature. The image lives in us as a felt imperfection. To be human is to exist with the sense of an absence to be filled. Only in the light of our human substance's longing for union with the divine do our lesser yearnings make sense. Only the eternal Logos will order these yearnings well and draw them out of chaos into *kosmos*.

The magnitude of the notion that created matter might become a vehicle for divine self-revelation is brought out in a splendid ancient text: a *midrash*, or paraphrastic commentary, on the first chapters of Genesis known as *The Cave of Treasures*. It was composed in Syriac, extant from the fourth century. Hardly anyone reads it any more, at least not in the West. An English translation was published by the Religious Tracts Society in the early twentieth century, furnished with an apologetic preface by the Orientalist Ernest Wallis Budge, who remarked,

> On the historical facts which form the framework of the *CT*, the pious author grafted a series of legends, many of which deserve the descriptions of idle stories and vain fables. The reader will understand that such legends are neither accepted nor endorsed by any member of the Society or by myself. These legends were inserted with the view of making the *CT* a sort of religious 'wonder-book' which would appeal to the vivid *&* credulous imaginations of Christian natives in almost every country of the Near East.

We, like Budge, pride ourselves on being cleverer than 'credulous natives'. You may ask why I propose to contaminate you with discredited nonsense, albeit venerable.

I am doing so on good authority. If we leap a century forward in time and consult a monograph by Su-Min Ri, the Korean scholar who in 1987 published the edited Syriac text of *The Cave of Treasures* after decades of research, we shall find him writing in the *Orientalia Christiania Analecta*, a publication not given to careless conjectures: 'On the basis of textual parallels, we take it for granted that St Ephrem knew *The Cave* by heart even before his Christian faith was consolidated. Only thus could he have used it as he did in all his works.' Su-Min Ri further identifies echoes in Irenaeus, Justin, Melito of Sardis and Julius Africanus. Closer to ourselves, we know it was a text in whose wake Milton sailed, drawn by its timeless fascination.

The Cave of Treasures speaks in terms foreign to post-Enlightenment sensibilities. Reading it, we must expect the unexpected. We have before us, though, a text that was a source for some of the Church's acutest minds. Therefore we should not dismiss it offhand. As we enter its world, we must abandon our customary chase for tidy definitions. We must be willing to think in images, to hear in symphony, as contrasting voices unite in novel harmonies. If we do, we shall find sophisticated literature. We shall see human origins, the human condition and human finality in a new perspective. In the Genesis narrative, we shall recognize ourselves.

This is how *The Cave* recounts what took place on the sixth day of creation:

On the sixth day, which is Friday, at the first hour, while silence reigned over all the powers of the orders of spiritual beings, God said: 'Let us make man in our image, as our resemblance,' indicating by the [letter] *nun*, instead of the *alaf*, the glorious persons of the Son and the Spirit. When the angels heard this word, they were seized with terror and said among themselves: 'A great wonder has appeared to us today, the resemblance of God, our Maker.' And they saw the right hand of God, which took dust from the earth, which is to say from the four elements: the hot and the cold, the dry and the moist. Why did God make Adam from these four feeble elements?

In order that, by them, all that is in him might be subject to him. And God fashioned Adam with his holy hands, as his image. When the angels saw his glorious aspect, they were troubled on account of the beauty of his likeness.

The silence of the spheres summons up creation's expectancy as God prepared to produce the being for whom all other things had been made. In the plural form of the Biblical phrase, 'Let us make' (which in Hebrew can simply be a way of expressing deliberation), *The Cave of Treasures* detects a reference to the Blessed Trinity. From the point of view of Christian theology, this makes sense. The triune nature of God was revealed and became susceptible of articulation in the wake of the incarnation, but its reality is eternal, preceding creation. The image in which human substance was formed is a trinitarian image, relational in essence.

You Are What You Wear

The Cave of Treasures, I have said, is a *midrash*. The noun derives from the root דרש [*darash*], which means to scrutinize. In rabbinic tradition it indicated a method of interpretation that goes beyond the literal sense of Scripture to examine the text in every aspect, squeezing out each drop of sense in order to apply this essence to the needs of believers. The concern of *The Cave of Treasures* is the life (and afterlife) of Adam, the first-formed human being. His life is a paradigm of our existence, yours and mine. The text offers a sweep of world history from the beginning of creation to Christ's resurrection, dated to the year 5,500.

Adam's story is told in terms of metaphors of clothing, of a series of garments put on and taken off. This is less odd than it may at first seem. If we look closely, we find the motif of dressing to be central in Genesis 1-3. Western painting and literature tend only to recall Adam's self-made fig-leaf apron. But this is but one of several vestments in the story. At the end of Genesis 3, when Adam and Eve are expelled from the Garden, the Lord puts on them 'garments of skin' that he, God, has made (3.21). Before the Fall, too, they were somehow dressed, for otherwise how could they suddenly, upon having sinned, have discovered nakedness?

The Syriacs interpreted these primordial clothes in the light of the Psalter. Where in our Hebrew-based Bibles Psalm 8.6 reads, 'You made him little less than angels; with glory and honour you crowned him' (וְכָבוֹד וְהָדָר תְּעַטְּרֵהוּ), the Syriac Old Testament read, 'with glory and honour you *clothed* him.' The Syriac Fathers found in this verb a reference to the original innocence of Adam and Eve. Thus arose a splendid image, crucial to St Ephrem: that of the 'robes of glory' which our parents wore at first.

We are presented with a protological sequence dramatically paced with reference to items from a wardrobe: from original glory-clothes through the trauma of nakedness to the subterfuge of leaf aprons to garments of skin made by God. It will be worth our while to consider these items in turn.

When the Lord proclaimed his intention to make the human being in his image the angels trembled. These transcendent beings, assigned to stand watch before God's countenance singing his glory, were seized with fear at the thought that uncreated splendour should reside in a created being. Even before Adam was formed, the angels exclaimed, 'A great wonder has appeared to us today, the likeness of God, our Creator.' The thought alone was awesome.

When God proceeded to form man with his right hand, he made him from the four created elements: heat and cold, dryness and moisture. Another wonder: making an image of himself, why would God make use of such beggarly stuff? He did it so that, by them, all things would be subject to man and show their purpose through him. Adam is a microcosm. He contains in himself the elements of all that exists. Thereby he stands in necessary kinship with creation. In him, dust and glory are conjoined in continuous extension from earth to heaven.

'When the angels saw his glorious aspect, they were troubled by the beauty of his likeness.' The still, supine form moved: Adam stretched and stood up. Even his stature, resolutely vertical, pointed him heavenward. God caused the animals to pass before him to be named, 'while they inclined their heads and adored him'. Then He led him into Eden, to serve 'as a priest in Holy Church'.

The exaltation of Adam's first glory is evidenced by its contrast with what follows. The events of the fall, well known, are recounted without melodrama in *The Cave*. Thereby the objective tragedy is made more apparent. It is not so much Adam's guilt that is brought to the fore as his existential poverty. He discovers, all at once, that his life is contingent. He sees that what he took for granted – familiarity with God, the glorious robe, lordship over creation – was not his by right; it was pure grace, lost, now, through his own betrayal. Disobedience shattered the life-bestowing bond of trust that was his lifeline to divinity.

Adam in the Garden, at the centre of a triptych that connects him
both with God and with the animal kingdom. Of course, he is
still waiting for Eve, lodged within him. Painted by the Ukrainian
iconographer Lyuba Yatskiv. © ICONART Gallery.

Fallen Adam finds himself reduced to elemental nature. Where before he had stood in a wonderful tension, *of* the earth but straining towards heaven, he is subject now to the crushing downward pull of gravity. He is drawn towards earth, towards death, towards the grave. *That* is the cause of his shame: to have lowered himself so far underneath the dignity that was his first lot. His once resplendent body has become a 'body of grief' weighed down by needs and passions. Covering himself with matter, Adam strives to maintain decorum, yet more essentially he hides. He wants to merge with material creation from which he no longer stands out. Having forfeited likeness to God, what else could he do? Where else could he look for solidarity, security and, quite simply, distraction?

In the account of Adam's fall that has formed western consciousness, the story seems to end here. This is where we customarily take leave of Adam, naked, ashamed, pathetically robed. We look at him with embarrassment, the way we might see a disreputable old uncle we would rather excise from the family tree. *The Cave of Treasures* reminds us, though, that the story is far from finished.

Even before Adam fell for the serpent's deceit, we are told, 'God presciently knew what Satan had plotted, so placed [Adam] in his mercy beforehand, as blessed David sings, "Lord, you have been for us from age to age a house in which to dwell," which is to say, You have made us in your mercy.' The Scripture cited is Psalm 89.1. In the *Grail Psalter* it reads, 'O Lord, you have been our refuge.'

How are we to see the application of this well-known text to this unfamiliar context? *The Cave of Treasures* ascribes to the relationship between God and man a second original dimension, a dimension beyond, yet able to contain, the familiar dichotomy of first innocence *versus* subsequent guilt. The truth of the Adam we meet in this text is not adequately defined by the fall. The fall itself is mysteriously held by grace. This meaning is epically brought out when the time comes for Adam to be expelled from paradise. The Genesis account is stern, ringing with imprecations. Centuries of moralist preaching have accustomed us to think God angry, booting Adam out. The tradition of the *Cave* presents a different picture. Here, Adam is led to Eden's gate with consoling words. God grieves at the leave-taking, but urges Adam not to despair. 'Adam, do not be distressed', he says,

> that you must, on account of the sentence, depart from Paradise. I will bring you back to your inheritance! See how I have loved you! On your account I have cursed the earth, but you I have spared from curses. Since you *have* transgressed, do leave, but do not be distressed. For when time has been fulfilled, I will send my Son, and by my Son your salvation will be wrought.

A later, Arabic version adds: 'I have clothed you with my mercy.'

The God-given garments of skin are a mercy-cover, a sacrament of kindness. Though stripped of glory, Adam proceeds wrapped in grace. This vesture will give him the comfort and fortitude he needs to till and toil while awaiting redemption. It protects Adam's present existence, safeguarding his iconic nature in a setting of estrangement. The promise of deliverance will illumine humanity's exile. From the first, Adam is told, 'You must go forth from me, but I will bring you back.' God *is* for him a refuge. Adam is a stranger on the earth, yes, but a shielded, sheltered stranger. He can hold his head high, not for proud self-assurance, but for God's assurance of love. He is a bearer of hope, the herald of a covenant of grace.

Thus reassured he can set forth from Eden, which according to *The Cave of Treasures* lies on the summit of a mountain reaching 'above all other mountains and higher than them by 300 spans by the spirit of the air'. Paradise is part of the cosmic order we know, yet at the same time set above it. It looms there in seclusion, not menacingly, but beckoning. 'For Eden', the text goes on, 'is a type of the true Church. And the Church is the mercy of God that is to spread itself over all mankind.'

LIFE OUTSIDE EDEN

Adam has known God's mercy. His task, and the task of his descendants, will be to draw that paradisal mercy down upon the world like a protective firmament. Once expelled from Eden, Adam settles on its outskirts, a short way down the mountain. God directs him to a cave there. It is to be for him a place of worship and waiting. There he is to serve as priest. Adam blesses the cave and puts in it frankincense, gold and myrrh collected from the edge of paradise, signs of blessedness known and lost awhile to which he aspires to return. In the fullness of time, the Magi's prophetic gifts will make it clear that this return is finally at hand.

Adam's cave outside paradise's walls becomes a second image of the Church, the Church in exile, we might say, or the pilgrim Church. Here Adam dies and is buried, having first instructed his sons to heed a God-given command: when at a future time they leave the mountain they must not abandon Adam's bones. They are to bring his body and re-bury it in the middle of the earth, where man's salvation will be wrought. Adam's sons promise to do as they were told. They pass the instruction down through generations, even as their number up near the cave declines.

The greater part of humanity is pulled further and further down the mountain, away from the scents and sounds of paradise. The story of our race is presented as the story of a gradual downward sliding from the open views of the heights towards the lowlands, inhabited by Cain since the fratricide, the haunt of self-seeking, self-absorbed mankind. One by one, the mountain dwellers descend, drawn by lust, curiosity and appetite. Once they merge with the dwellers of the plain, they find they cannot re-scale the mountain. Its rocks turn into fire.

For a while, however, human beings *were* able to maintain, even in this world of tears, a life patterned on the life of paradise. They remembered. They worshipped. They prayed in the cave, recalling Adam's origins, his fall, then the mercy that sustained him. With time, memory faded, and with it the yearning to return to beatitude. By the end of the first millennium, we are told, only Noah and his sons were left within reach of the cave. There they built the Ark. In the middle of it, like an altar, they installed Adam's body, surrounded by the paradisal gold, frankincense and myrrh. When waters of retribution swelled upon the earth, the Ark rose. It hovered for a moment in the air. It turned north, then south; then, again from the middle, east and west, blessing the flood with the cruciform and saving sign. Then it sailed. And the world was submerged in its baptism of death, in the hope of new life.

The middle of the earth, where Adam was to be interred, is Golgotha, of course. The rest of the text briskly sums up the course of the world until Christ's redemption. Christ's Passion seals humanity's call, symbolically put before us in the itinerary of Adam. Strikingly, the symbolic framework of *The Cave of Treasures* intersects with imagery well known to us. It is common, in Northern Europe, for pictures of the Crucified to feature a skull underneath the cross. That skull is not generic. It is Adam's, which had known the touch of God's hands and been crowned with glory. When blood and water trickled from Christ's side, we read in *The Cave*, they flowed into Adam's mouth. God's promise was fulfilled. Adam was saved, after waiting for millennia. By a decree of restitution drawn up in Christ's blood, he was restored to freedom from death's dungeon.

At that point, the garment of skin could be shed. The robe of glory was available to clothe humanity anew. The two Adams, old and new, could meet in an embrace, father and Son, son and Father. The tree of the cross is revealed as the axis on which the world turns. Christ shows us Adam's true face. Contemplating Christ, we see what man was meant to be: *Ecce homo*! *The Cave of Treasures* sets out their intertwining destinies in a masterful Two-Part Invention:

At the first hour of Friday, God formed Adam from dust; and at the first hour of Friday, Christ was spat on by the cursed sons of his crucifiers. At the third hour of Friday, the crown of glory was placed on Adam's head; and at the third hour of Friday, the crown of thorns was placed on the head of Christ. At the sixth hour, Eve gave Adam the fruit of bitterness of death. At the sixth hour, the assembly of the lawless gave Christ vinegar and bile. For three hours, Adam stood stripped under the tree. And for three hours Christ hung naked on wood. From Adam's left side, Eve came forth, the mother of mortal children. From Christ's right side

baptism emerged, the mother of children who will not
see death. On Friday Adam and Eve sinned. And on
Friday their sin was forgiven. On Friday Adam and Eve
were stripped. And on Friday Christ stripped himself
and re-clothed them. At the ninth hour of Friday,
Adam went down to the low-lying earth from the
heights of Paradise. And at the ninth hour of Friday,
Christ went down into the lower regions of the earth
from the height of the Cross, to visit those who lay
in the dust. In all things, Christ was made similar to
Adam, as it is written.

This text points forward to the lovely recitative at the end
of Bach's St Matthew Passion, *Am Abend, da es kühle war*.
After the unbearable tension of Jesus's suffering and death,
this piece is redolent with peace. It conveys caressing
tenderness. The cry, 'It is accomplished,' sung by the solo
bass, means exactly what it says. Christ rests. We also can
rest. The world's trauma is healed. Even as Adam's fall
was revealed at nightfall, the dove returned to the Ark
at even-time, and now, *this* evening, our peace is made
with God. 'O lovely time!' Such parallelism, expounded
by the Fifth Evangelist, presupposes the tradition we
have considered. It affords a profound understanding of
Christ's saving work understood as reconciliation.

Still more importantly, it takes us to the heart of the
Christian condition. For if the story of Adam is told
with such care it is because his story is ours. We, too,
must negotiate its various stages. To make this statement
concrete, let me cite another ancient text, again of Syriac
origin. It is a liturgical blessing, pronounced over the
neophyte ascending from the full-immersion baptistry.
The manuscript it stems from is seventh-century, but the

prayer is certainly older. It takes *The Cave*'s theology for granted. If you would hear the full force of it, try reading it out aloud:

> O brother! Sing praise to the Son of the Lord of all, who has made for you a crown more desirable than that of any king. Brilliant is your garment, brother, like the sun: and your face shines like an angel's. Like an angel you rose up, beloved, from the baptistry by the power of the Holy Spirit. Brother, you have been granted access to the wedding chamber. Today you have put on anew the glory of Adam. Your garments are lovely, your crown beautiful. By the ministry of his priest, the Firstborn has prepared them for you. The fruit Adam did not taste in Paradise has been placed, today, in your mouth. Go in peace, son of the baptistry. Adore the Cross! It will preserve you.

In baptism, we, too, dead in sin, have, like Adam, been touched by the life-giving stream flowing from Christ's side. We have been raised up and restored. We possess, in potential, the glory from which our father fell. The drama of our Christian life scintillates with glory. It is a drama of breathtaking dimensions. It requires us, at once, to recall our first origins and final end as we lay claim to the truth of our being, showered with grace in the communion of Christ's Church, which is, as we have seen, 'the mercy of God spreading itself over all mankind'.

A text like *The Cave of Treasures* offers us a privileged way of *entering* salvation by its resolute appeal to experience. The Christian proclamation can easily become rather abstract. This is more the case today than in the recent past, as Christian terminology is increasingly emptied of specific meaning. It is hard to present the Gospel on the terms, say, of the Letter to the Romans to people who shake their heads at the very notion of 'sin', see no need for 'expiation', so cannot conceive of what 'redemption' is good for, never mind 'sanctification'.

The tendency of our time is to idealize nature, with its impulses and appetites, not to transcend it. While anthropological discourse since antiquity has dwelt on what sets man apart from other species, there is a strange determination abroad, these days, to evidence that we are no more than animals.

This does not mean, though, that our age is impervious to the Spirit. The claims of the soul are evident for being often expressed negatively, a function of pain. While moderns are loath to speak of God, they readily admit to feeling trapped in creaturely limitation. While giving no explicit credence to doctrines of the afterlife, they are consumed with a yearning for *more*. While determined to assume their incarnate humanity, they vaguely know that our body points beyond itself, since every apparent satisfaction is but achingly provisional.

The imaged anthropology of *The Cave of Treasures* will possibly go further in this world of ours, obsessed with images, than the admirable but austere definitions of scholastic theology. That is why I am keen to ground my reflection on chastity in the narrative of a dignified substance divinely adorned, then stripped of glory, reduced to a state of confused desire, ever wanting more than earthly life can provide yet able, even among thorns, to know moments of exultant joy, proceeding homeward – whether or not one knows where home is – robed in mercy.

Leaning on this narrative, deeply Scriptural, I will suggest that the wholeness to which a chaste ideal would lead is not contrary to nature but stands for nature's fulfilment. It is an ideal sprung from our gracious origin and pointing towards our supernatural end. The pursuit of integrity is rarely straightforward. It can take us through momentous tensions, which we shall consider. Still, it is a vital option, an option that stands a good chance of bringing happiness. In the language of Deuteronomy, it stands for the choice of life, not of death (Deuteronomy 30.15-20).

At first glance the anthropology of *The Cave of Treasures* may seem voluntarist and excessively affirmative: from glory to glory! We have noted, though, the depths to be plumbed between origin and end. The Adam we encounter in this environment is not the villain of radical Augustinianism, but nor is he a hapless victim. He is responsible. He owns responsibility. His story has the density of life really lived. He carries the mark of the fall, yes, of course, but he also remembers the fragrances of Paradise. And he is robed in mercy. This is the crucial insight.

Of Adam's four stages of growth in *The Cave of Treasures*, three are conceivable as symbols outside Gospel parameters. Secular anthropologies might accommodate an initial exposure, a fig-leaf disguise, and a finality of relative 'glory'. Popular narratives of human perfectibility are premised on gloriousness, be its bliss this-worldly. The Christian difference resides in mercy, in the obstinacy of pardoning grace, a quality of gentleness that shows itself to be, in the strict sense, essential.

Once we conceive of human life as potentially embraced and contained by mercy, we avoid three pitfalls: the optimist, progressivist creed of modernity whose refrains we rehearse and pass on, though with ever scanter conviction; the pessimist, despair-inducing hunch that the world is chronically sick and bound for self-destruction; and the fatalist, cynically detached vision that sees the world governed in any case by factors beyond our control – so why not just eat, drink, sleep around, be merry, and opt for oblivion?

The more we are aware of being robed in mercy, the more serenely we can live with ourselves, with our desires and flaws, contradictions and hopes. Mercy gives us courage to remember and look forward. It enables pardon, gives strength for compassion, nurtures hope. The Christian mission is to spread mercy abroad, to let no corner of the world, no single tear-stained destiny, remain untouched by it. The Adam we contemplate, in whom we see ourselves, is at once a teacher of truth and a witness to mercy. He unravels the fullness of our human state in its tragedy *and* in its glory. Of these, the latter aspect is the more crucial. His desire is fixed on Jesus even before he knows who the promised Saviour is. He is an *alter ego* with whom we can be reconciled. He can take us by the hand, for he knows where we are going.

Among the spiritual giants of the twentieth century was a man steeped in the spirit of *The Cave of Treasures*, a compassionate man who understood that spirit, lived by it and passed it on. I have in mind St Silouan of Mount Athos (1866–1938), described by Thomas Merton as the most authentic monk of the twentieth century. As a conclusion to this chapter and a prelude to the next, I wish to share a passage from his prose poem 'Adam's Lament'. It speaks of our journey through this world, made up of longing and labour, comfort and hardship, love and loneliness, repentance and praise, resonant with the echo of heavenly harmony. Further, it invites us to

make peace with our origin and so, by implication, with
ourselves.

I write of thee, O Adam;
But thou art witness, my feeble understanding
cannot fathom thy longing after God,
nor how thou didst carry the burden of repentance.
O Adam, thou dost see how I, thy child, suffer here
on earth.
Small is the fire within me,
and the flame of my love flickers low.
O Adam, sing unto us the song of the Lord,
that my soul may rejoice in the Lord,
and be moved to praise and glorify him
as the cherubim and seraphim praise him in the
heavens,
and all the hosts of heavenly angels sing to him the
thrice-holy hymn.
O Adam, our father, sing unto us the Lord's song,
that the whole earth may hear,
and all thy sons may lift their minds to God
and delight in the strains of the heavenly anthem,
and forget their sorrows on earth . . .
O Adam, comfort and cheer our troubled souls.

Tensions

Of the three states of being which *The Cave of Treasures* presents, two are known to us experientially: the state of nakedness (of living with the wound of sin, in death's shadow), and the state of being clothed in 'garments of skin' (of living within an economy of mercy). The sacramentally pledged state of being robed in glory is known to us only by virtue of faith-filled hope.

This hope is illumined by a flicker of ontological remembrance. We perceive it in both body and mind, variously with delight and with pain, as a yearning for infinity. But we do not, now, *know* what it was like to subsist in a prelapsarian nature formed by God's hands and quickened by his breath, functioning according to a God-like structure; nor do we *know* what it will be like for this structure to find itself restored by redemptive grace in eternal life, in Christ.

This fact poses a conundrum we cannot suavely farm out to ivory-tower theologians. It concerns us intimately. In existential terms we might state it like this: we do not, in fact, know what is natural to us. Therefore we struggle to live naturally. In Christian terms, the natural state of man is to subsist in the divine image and to correspond to God's likeness. This harmonious subsistence was brought to an end through the event we refer to as the Fall. As a result of it, human nature, made for immortality, found itself restricted by the necessity of death, caught up in the wheels of calculable time. As Panayotis Nellas has written in an important book,

> experience proves that the historical reality of man is different from that which we have seen to be defined by the phrase 'in the image'. In the Christian perception of things this is to be ascribed to the fact that the historical reality develops within the unnatural situation in which man has found himself since the fall.

For us, it does seem 'natural' to be governed by instincts and physical necessities, to suffer, decay and die, realities symbolized and held by the garments of skin. Yet in terms of our nature's intended purpose and potential, these factors are anomalous. What *is* natural is to be governed by the Word, and thereby to know, in God, freedom, harmony and joy. More or less consciously, human beings seek a way back to life as it was before. Our quests for knowledge, development, justice, freedom and the rest, says Nellas, are in roundabout ways 'quests for [humankind's] iconic nature'.

> Experience, however, proves again that humanity does not find today what it seeks. This, in the Christian view of things, is not because it is impossible for humanity to find these things, or because they do not belong to it, but because it begins from a false starting point and a mistaken orientation. The false starting point is the failure to appreciate the unnatural condition in which

we find ourselves, and the mistaken orientation is that we are searching for something which is natural in the midst of what is unnatural. What is naturally good for man can be found if it is sought at its real source, and if man in order to find it makes full use of his natural powers.

As long as we construct our lives on a merely empirical basis, we shall carry on mistaking what is provisional for that which endures. A broadening of perspective is required, not to dismiss the provisional – for it is precious – but to evaluate it rightly, to learn not to expect it to yield what it cannot. Our deep experience must be drawn back to 'its real source' and oriented well if we truly wish to thrive. With this in mind, we may consider certain tensions apt to mark our quest for affective and sexual integrity; that is, for chastity.

BODY AND SOUL

In Norwegian historiography, the Battle of Stiklestad has the epic resonance of the Battle of Hastings. It was pitched on 29 July 1030. In the course of it, King Olav Haraldsson, freshly returned from exile spent in what is now Ukraine, was killed with an axe. His death was a cruel blow to the faction he had led, which had no obvious new figurehead. The king was sorely mourned. His body was washed and laid out. Then something strange happened. The hagiographical *Passio Olavi*, written a century and a half later, describes the incident as follows:

When the time of Olav's passion was ended and the king's servants had washed his sacred body in a hut, the water, mixed with the holy martyr's blood, was poured out in front of the door. A blind man who happened to pass that house slid at the place still wet with the blood-and-water mixture. When the man touched his eyes with wet fingers, his darkness disappeared at once and he got back the sight he had earlier enjoyed. Astonished, he who had experienced this divine miracle set about finding out where the blood came from that had been mingled with the water. He learned that it must have been by merit of the holy martyr Olav that he had regained sight. All who heard tell of this miracle marvelled, praising God and his love for having chosen to make his martyr known by means of such an unusual miracle.

From then on, Olav's body occasioned many miracles. It was perceived as a conduit of grace, conveying in its materiality the fruits of a sanctified life. Olav's body manifested his Christ-configured soul, purified through trials to become a mirror apt to reflect God's healing mercy. People came in droves to pray beside the body, to see it and touch it. What is more, though Olav was manifestly dead, his body showed continued signs of organic life: the bishop of Nidaros (medieval Trondheim) had to keep cutting his hair and nails, 'for both grew as when he was a man fully alive in this world'. The national unity which Olav had been unable to establish while alive gradually formed around his incorrupt body and the cult that ensued.

Countless variations on this story could be told from all over Christendom, by no means only from the mist-shrouded distant past. Edgar Alison Peers, professor of Spanish at Liverpool for decades until his death in 1952, shares a memory about his friend Dom Edmund Gurdon, the English Carthusian who served as prior of Miraflores in Spain. One day, Gurdon had sent two brothers out to dig a grave for a monk who had just died. After a short while, the brothers burst into Dom Edmund's cell, terribly excited. They were carrying a spade on which there were fresh bloodstains. The prior thought at first there had been an accident.

> But when they could speak coherently they told him that they had dug down to a depth of about 6 feet, when one of their spades struck against something soft and, when it was pulled out, had blood on it. Very much astonished, they put it down, and with their spades gradually uncovered the body of a young man. There was no sign of his habit, nor of any planks, but his tonsure was there, and blood was running from a wound in his arm. 'He looked as if he was asleep.' They had left him untouched, and come to tell Dom Edmund so that he should see the miracle.

The modern narrative mirrors the medieval. We might expect, next, commotion, wonder-hunger, even a degree of self-advertising display. There was none of it. Dom Edmund told his brothers that he did not intend to go to the cemetery. 'Of course, I believed them,' he said. 'I would have done so even if there had not been blood on the spade.'

'What did you do?'

'I said, there are many saints in the Carthusian Order. Cover him up again and give him a cross, so that he won't be disturbed any more.'

For Dom Edmund, a supremely rational, supernaturally minded Englishman, the phenomenon the brothers had met in the graveyard was exceptional, yes, but not abnormal. On the contrary, it stood for what ought to be a Christian norm. It is not man's spiritual faculties alone that have been made in the image of God, but his physical being also. Christian belief in the resurrection of the *flesh* presupposes the body's potential and call to resist corruption.

This has always been a stumbling block to unbelievers, indeed to some believers, too. The notion of the *soul's* immortality appeals even in a post-Christian age. We like the thought that something about us carries on somehow after we are dead and gone. The vague associations evoked by the word 'soul' represent an idealized projection of what we might think of as our noblest self. The thought of the body's immortality, meanwhile, is widely met with ridicule. For all our body-consciousness we are keen, when the time comes, to leave our bodies behind.

The body does, though, point beyond itself. It carries a hunger, not just for sensual satisfaction, but for eternity. A splendid Psalm (Psalm 62), which David sang out in the Judaean desert hiding from Saul, begins with this visceral confession:

> O God, you are my God, I seek you, my soul thirsts for you; my flesh faints for you, as in a dry and weary land where no water is.

The Vulgate, which has shaped Christian consciousness in the West, renders the notion of the flesh's fainting differently, and suggestively, by the exclamation: '*quam multipliciter tibi caro mea!*' (following the LXX's

ποσαπλῶς σοι ἡ σάρξ μου): 'in what multiple ways my
flesh tends towards you', or even, 'in what multiple ways
my flesh is yours'. There is imprinted on our physical
being a craving that is, as T. S. Eliot put it in *The Rock*,
'Crying for life beyond life, for ecstasy not of the flesh'.

It is hard to entertain a chaste approach to the body if
we have a reductive understanding of that of which the
body is capable; if we reduce a dimension of ourselves
configured to the image of God simply to a discardable
garment of skin. We carefully, sometimes obsessively,
attend to the body's present needs, appetites and pains.
But are we not often deaf to its crying out for ways to
transcend itself while staying fully itself? Are we not
closed to the thought that our senses' claims may call for
something that cannot be found in this world?

To say this is not to denigrate the here-and-now
of sensual experience, or to recommend exsanguine
sublimation patterned on a dualist frame of mind. It is to
root the supernatural in nature, *our* nature, and thereby
to broaden (infinitely) the range of desire. Only thus can
we learn to seek proportionate responses to what our flesh
faints for and spare ourselves repeated frustration.

Naturally, erotic intimacy can be one way of tending
towards the sublime. The testimonies of lovers abound
from every age and cultural sphere. Certain narratives
posit sensual awakening as a corrective to an arid spiritual
search turned in on itself to become subtle self-satisfaction.
A parable of this process is told in Hermann Hesse's novel
Siddhartha. After a noviciate spent among ascetics, the
eponymous hero rediscovers the world and is, for the first
time, touched by it thanks to the wise courtesan Kamala.
Entranced by her beauty, he is tempted, first, to see her as
a trophy to be conquered, even ravished. Kamala corrects

him: 'Love can be begged for, bought, given, found on the
street, but you cannot take it as spoil. The way you have
thought out for yourself is quite wrong.'

It takes her to teach him what reciprocity means, and
surrender. She draws him out of self-centred existence
into an experience at once of encounter and ecstasy:

> She taught him, who in the things of love was still a boy
> tending to throw himself blindly and insatiably into
> pleasure as into an abyss – she taught him from scratch
> the doctrine that one can't take pleasure without at the
> same time giving it; that every gesture, every caress,
> every touch, every look, each smallest spot on the body
> carries secrets the awakening of which paves the way to
> happiness for those in the know. She taught him that
> lovers can't part after celebrating love without admiring
> each other, without having been conquered in the
> measure in which they themselves have conquered, so
> that neither is subject to a surfeit or to boredom or to
> the ugly sense of having abused or been abused.

For Siddhartha this insight marks a crucial stage on the
journey to enlightenment. He could have reached it
otherwise, but this path opened up before him.

Much as he enjoyed following it, he was never inclined
to mistake it for a goal. He ascertains the troubling
proximity of lust and death. And he perceives, even in
Kamala, a hidden fear: 'fear of ageing, fear of the autumn,
fear of having to die'. He recognizes the loveliness of that
which they have known together. But he sees that it cannot
be an end in itself. It is evidently transitory, whereas both
he and Kamala yearn to embody a beauty that endures.

The human will to embody beauty is, I suspect, under-rated. But it lives in us as a consequence and expression of our iconic nature. He in whose image we are made *is* Beauty. Beauty is naturally the end towards which we strive. An echo of this striving is heard, no doubt, in our times' focus on fitness and good looks. But beauty is about more than being pressed into shape. Beauty is a function of art. Art must be carefully practised and deliberately refined. It seeks expression.

For years I have been haunted by a throwaway statement in Tim Winton's weird, in some ways perverse, novel *Breath*. One of its characters sees, looking back over life, that he awoke to a new dimension of being one day in adolescence, out on an Australian beach, when he noticed surfers riding a wave. It was new to him: 'I couldn't have put words to it as a boy, but later I understood what seized my imagination that day. How strange it was to see men do something beautiful. Something pointless and elegant, as though nobody saw or cared.'

To do something beautiful for its own sake, for the intrinsic delight of it, without thought of gain: this, I'd say, is a way of beginning to live chastely in this world, poised to balance elegantly on whatever surging billow providence provides as a means to bear us homeward, towards the shore.

Could it be, as Winton suggests, that such gratuitous seeing and acting in pursuit of beauty is *stranger* to men than it is to women?

Perhaps no form of concrete human enterprise grants a premonition of the body's possible ascent towards transcendent beauty more clearly than dance, an art form in which iron discipline enables, over time, breathtaking

freedom of expression. The reclusive Norwegian poet
Emil Boyson framed this ascent in words:

Dét at du finnes i verden, gjør at livet kan leves.
Du er den skjulte sangfugl, du er nymånens skjønnhet,
du er den hvite lengsels-sky, du er hvirvelstormen
som river oss ut av oss selv og lærer vor søte smerte
at Alt skal skiftes om lik et klædebon, og at éngang,
når skjebnens mål er fullt, må denne jords åsyn forgå.

Hvem skulle tro at DU, som holder i din hånd
de ytterste hemmeligheter, kjent ellers av Gud alene,
selv er en sky ung pike, som tusen passérer på gaten
og ingen vet annet om enn at du liker kryss-ord,
tørrer støv for din mor, taler fornuftig om været,
og strikker små trøier til barnet din søster venter i mars!

Ræddes du aldri, når natten er tyst, for ditt væsens gåde?
Blev det vor lodd at gruble, fordi din panne er klar?
—Hva vet du om spørsmål og svar! Du smiler og går forbi
mot virkelighetens grense, forunderlig ett med din skjebne,
og mens vore hjerter sitrer, forvandler du dig pånytt
og finner, fortapt i en frihet du aldri har prøvd at fatte,
benådelsens strenge mønster som er blitt ett med din kropp,
og synker sammen som død når din siste dans er til-ende.

Life is made bearable because, in this world, you exist.
You are the hidden songbird. You are the new moon's
beauty.
You are the white cloud of yearning. You are the
tornado that
pulls us out of ourselves and lets our sweet pain know
that all will be changed like a garment and that one day

when fate's measure is full the face of this world must
pass.

Who would have thought that YOU, who hold in your
hand
ultimate secrets known otherwise to God alone,
should be a shy young girl whom thousands pass in
the street,
about whom nought is known except that you like
crosswords,
do housework for your mother, speak sense about the
weather,
and knit little vests for the child your sister expects in
March.

Are you never fearful, in the quiet of the night, of your
being's enigma?
Is it your unfurrowed brow that obliges us to brood?
What do you know of questions and answers? You
smile as you pass
on your way to reality's frontier, strangely united with
your fate;
while our hearts quiver you are again transformed,
finding, lost in a freedom you have never sought to
fathom,
the rigorous paradigm of grace made one with your
body,
then collapsing as if dead at the end of your last dance.

In such performance we intuit the work of unification we
are called to effect, reconciled to our fate, as grace's pattern is
made one with our body, bearing us beautifully up towards
the boundary of all that is.

'You are the tornado/pulling us out of ourselves and letting our sweet pain know/that all will be changed like a garment and that one day/ when fate's measure is full the face of this world must pass.' How little Virginia Woolf had understood when she ridiculed a famous ballerina of her day for spending life 'hopping about from foot to foot'.

MALE AND FEMALE

In current usage 'sex' is variously an activity, a commodity and a compulsion. One can 'have' it, 'buy' it, be 'addicted to' it. Etymologically speaking, 'sex' refers to a state of being. The Latin noun *sexus* derives from *seco*, which means 'to cut off' or 'to amputate'. The same root gives us 'secateurs'. *Sexus* refers to the division of a species into two kinds, male and female, each incomplete without the other. By extension it came to denote the sexual organs. Only fairly recently was it adopted as the direct object of verbs denoting human endeavour.

Genesis does derive gender difference from a sort of amputation. The story of it crowns the creation narrative. From the initial 'Let there be light!' God had ordered reality by graceful distinctions, drawing light from darkness, earth from heaven, dry land from water, and so forth. When at last the scene was set and the earth was ready, he drew woman from man (Genesis 2.21-23):

> And the Lord God caused a deep sleep to fall upon Adam, and he slept: and he took one of his ribs, and closed up the flesh instead thereof; and the rib, which the Lord God had taken from man, made he a woman, and brought her unto the man. And Adam said, 'This is now bone of my bones, and flesh of my flesh: she shall be called Woman, because she was taken out of Man.'

These resonant cadences from the King James Bible convey the moment's solemnity. The Hebrew text, meanwhile, has a dimension we might call playful, an expression of astonished delight. When Adam awakens from sleep, he cries out,

זֹאת הַפַּעַם עֶצֶם מֵעֲצָמַי וּבָשָׂר מִבְּשָׂרִי לְזֹאת יִקָּרֵא אִשָּׁה כִּי מֵאִישׁ לֻקֳחָה-זֹּאת

Martin Buber, a formidable Hebraist, renders this verse: 'Now this time round, here she is! Bone of my bones, flesh of my flesh. Ishah shall be her name for from Ish

she was drawn.' I do not think it disrespectful to compare
the Biblical Adam's stuttered naming of this well-known
stranger ('Ish-Ish-ah') to the 'Pa-Pa-ge' duet at the end
of *The Magic Flute*, when Papageno falls at last into the
embrace of her whom, so far, he has only known as a
gnawing sense of absence. The Mozartian heroes are also
paradisal creatures of a kind.

In both symbolic narratives, man and woman meet
with a loud exclamation of 'Yes!' Having sought his mate
in vain in the range of creatures coming before him to be
named, Adam knows her when he sees her, roused from
his first siesta. The sole insufficiency of life in Eden is
blissfully repaired. He is no longer alone.

Rashi of Troyes, a contemporary of the founders of
Cîteaux, remarks that the Hebrew noun conventionally
rendered 'rib' (צֵלָע), suggesting the formation of
woman from man's bare bones, is susceptible of a
different reading. The same noun is used, he points
out, in the Exodus account that reveals to Moses the
pattern for the tabernacle, God's earthly dwelling,
when it is said: 'And for the second side (צֶלַע) of the
tabernacle, on the north side, [you shall make] twenty
boards' (Exodus 26.20). 'For this reason our rabbis
have been able to say that man was created with two
faces.' Man and woman are intended to live face to
face. They are to affirm each other's personhood in
the relational, Greek sense of the word for person,
πρόσωπον [*prosōpon*], made up of πρός/*pros* ('towards')
and ὤψ/*ōps* ('eye'). I am a person in so far as I meet the
eye of another and the other's eye meets mine. As long
as man could not see himself in the eyes of woman, he
was but half a man.

Paul Claudel had valuable insight on this topic. In addition to being a poet, he was a careful exegete with an imaginative span at times as broad as Origen's:

'God created man in his own image: to the image of God he created him; male and female he created them.' The image of God exists by reason of this twofold nature. In Adam, the image of God, there was a latent something which in response to grace would give life to a woman. We do not read that God blew into Eve, as he did into Adam, 'a spirit of life'. This spirit was transmitted together with the portion of flesh which the hand of the Almighty set apart, which was no dead matter but living and alive. It is a bough cut off from the main stem. But the root remains in the depth of the male. And henceforth he has inside him something defined by an absence, a lack, a void that no flesh, nothing mortal can suffice to fulfil.

Drawing on the riches of the liturgy, Claudel adds a twist to this interdependence of the sexes. He refers to the fact that the Church, in its office for 8 December, the feast of the Immaculate Conception, lets us read a text from Proverbs. The reading likens Wisdom, the principle by which God acts in the world, to a woman, and insists that this figure was conceived before creation began: 'I was set up from everlasting, from the beginning, or ever the earth was. When there were no depths, I was brought forth' (Proverbs 8.23-24). Biblically speaking, writes Claudel, man may enjoy the status of being first-born, but woman was first conceived. 'And if she, the preordained figure of eternal Wisdom, is no stranger to the cause, creation and presence of any existing thing, she is no stranger to the raising-up of man.'

This may seem lovely but a bit unreal. You may find it tiresomely aestheticizing. Let us try, therefore, to root the poet's intuition in experience.

A testimony is at hand in a book by Jacques Lusseyran, the French resistance hero born in 1924, when Claudel was France's ambassador in Tokyo. Lusseyran, blind from the age of eight, is chiefly remembered for his visionary memoir, *And There Was Light*. Less well known is his *Conversation amoureuse*, a confession addressed to the woman he loved, Marie, a few months before the two died together in a car crash, on 27 July 1971. The *Conversation amoureuse* is an exceptional document, a searingly honest account of sexual experience, alive with light and joy. It steers liberatingly clear of the pornographic. Lusseyran, who only ever saw Marie with his heart and hands, was a man able to envisage sex chastely.

What Claudel inferred from Scripture, Lusseyran knew by instinct: 'I saw it when I was sixteen: I saw I would never be a man as long as I had not found woman.' Many a teenage boy might say the same, but Lusseyran had in mind more than erotic or romantic conquest; more, even, than the image of perfect love. His manhood, he sensed, depended on finding 'that part of *me* which is woman'.

Given current discourse about gender fluidity, we are perfectly set up to misunderstand what Lusseyran says. So let's not do that. He does not speak of identity conflict. His maleness was self-evident to him. He owned it with much pleasure. But he was keenly aware that being a man does not amount to self-sufficiency. On the contrary: for him, to be fully a man is to be humbly conscious of what one is *not*, to accept incompletion while passionately seeking

wholeness in – and from – the different other. It was clear
to Lusseyran that an individual becomes a person when
engaged in an ecstatic relationship; that is, in a relation
that makes me step outside myself in exposure to alterity:

> One cannot live imprisoned always. One cannot
> forever let life unfold on the other side of the fence.
> Human beings destroy one another. It is necessary, too,
> that they unite. It is urgent. There must be destinies
> that meet in an embrace. There must be a being, at
> least one, of whom one is never afraid, of whom one
> thinks as of oneself; who is sure of your protection, be
> it in the face of death, should death's prospect arise, a
> being whose eyes do not judge you, whose hands do
> not chase you away.

Such a statement has universal validity. It could be applied
to friendship. But it becomes a matter of life or death in
the male–female relationship. For man-without-woman,
and woman-without-man, is incomplete.

It is thought-provoking to read what Lusseyran wrote
about growing up in the 1930s, almost a century ago. 'I
wanted to be a boy. It didn't trouble me at all. Still, there
were times when I didn't quite feel like a boy, because
I couldn't be a girl at the same time.' Girls, he says,
saw things more clearly on the whole: 'Most said they
wished to be boys.' He concludes: 'It wasn't about being
otherwise. To become the opposite is never a solution. It
was about being both.'

How can this exacting, necessary union be effected?

First we must learn to recognize the terms of the
conflict within us. It is a tall order, for consciousness of
it arises in puberty, 'which is nothing but distance and

burning'. 'When one is very young, love hurts terribly. No one ever speaks of this, but it does hurt. Love bursts open in our sex and our head at the same time, pricking us, shouting at us, wanting the body at once.' It is, says Lusseyran, 'like a fire whose smoke clots our heart'. It provokes foolishness, even aggression. Woe to him or her who lives through this trying, intoxicating time without a friend to confide in.

As we grow, awakening is offered us: think of Adam's emerging from sleep. The question is whether we are ready and sufficiently free to seize this opportunity.

> In a flash, a boy knows that his body is no object, but a living being; and that a girl's body is another being still more alive, and so fragile that, were one mad enough to name its parts, one would shatter them. It is this embodied soul, this soul upon the body, that all, almost all, wish to forget. It frightens them.

Sexuality is more than a matter of physical need, physical functions. It is 'an overflowing, an inundation of soul'. It takes courage to recognize this fact. Lusseyran speaks of the promise held out by sexual union and of the disillusionment that *can* ensue. He stresses that his point of view is male, so partial. He hopes Marie will have 'like courage and speak of love as it is for a woman. It seems to me that it would be better for women to speak first; that they know more about it than we.'

With this condition in place, he submits that a man never dreams less than when he makes love, that at that moment he *is* what he *does* in a state of abandonment, and that for this reason it makes no sense to speak, as one did of old, of a man 'possessing' a woman. In reality, says Lusseyran, the opposite is true: he *gives* all. That is why, once the gift is symbolically given, he may fall into a state of desolation, even rage, confusedly attempting to maintain command of self where nothing seems to be left. Having been, briefly, one with the other, he falls back into separateness, well-known and troubling. At this point sadness can descend on a couple. There are those, Lusseyran admits, who may rise up and dance. But how many pray? The question is put, here, by one who is by no means overtly religious.

About his wife Lusseyran says a beautiful thing: 'All my movements are free; she has freed them.' Yet he acknowledges that there remains between them a gap of irremediable solitude. *She*, woman, incarnate in Marie, represents that without which he is not a man. The distance between them seems momentarily not to exist. Then it returns. That is when love is put to the test: 'It is after [the act of] love that love begins,' if each feels courageous and safe enough to acknowledge, having glimpsed completion through the other, that neither *is* complete; that it is tending beyond ourselves that makes us human. No one has a claim on completion. It can only be bestowed on us by way of fugitive gifts, for which we must be grateful:

It is about time we understood that there is in woman a man and in man a woman, and that each human being must work throughout life to know his or her name. Nothing, that is obvious, is gained by imitation. The day on which all boys pass as girls and all girls as boys, no progress will have been made. The distance to be covered cannot be reduced to the order of appearance. Nor to that of the professions. No claim [to equality] will open the door to the mystery. If each of us *is* the other in secret, the work must be done secretly. And only love can accomplish it.

'The decisive image', says Lusseyran to Marie, that towards which he tends, 'was not you, it was you in me', a transformative encounter enabling a fulfilment of self beyond self, in transformation. For love alters us. 'If our love keeps us as we were, it is because we mistook it for love, whereas in fact it was something else.'

Jacques Lusseyran's *Conversation amoureuse* gives us an idea, by no means exhaustive, but valuable all the same, of the way in which man and woman interact naturally. Sadly, their relationship has been upset. When Scripture speaks of the origin of sin, the first casualty is the natural, free relationship between the sexes. The fall lets Adam and Eve know what it means to be 'cut off'. They no longer find themselves in one another. They hide. They are ashamed.

When God calls them to account, his sanction affirms their estrangement. He says to the woman: 'Your desire shall be for your husband, and he shall rule over you' (Genesis 3.16). From this verse, a myth has grown. Readers – predominantly male readers – have deduced an image of needy and unbridled female sexuality, with woman cowering in the throes of desire at the feet of the providentially domineering male. This image was far from the mind of the inspired author. This is not just a hunch. It is an observation I can ground lexically.

The word used to render 'desire' in Genesis 3, תְּשׁוּקָה (*tshuqah*), is no common noun. It occurs only three times in the Hebrew Bible. This should prompt us to be on the alert: very likely there is a reason why the redactor adopted this term in this context, since its second occurrence is found just a few verses on (the third, apparently unrelated, is in a different book, the Song of Songs 7.11). In the protology, we find this particular 'desire' again in Genesis 4.7. There the Lord warns Cain of what will happen if he persists in an attitude of truculent rebellion, envying Abel instead of learning from his virtuous example. The Lord asks Cain why he sulks at the rejection of the offering he has brought:

> Why are you angry, and why has your countenance fallen? If you do well, will you not be accepted? And if you do not do well, sin is couching at the door; its desire [תְּשׁוּקָה] is for you, but you must master it (Genesis 4.6f.).

This usage puts paid to any notion of 'desire' as a state of dependent inferiority. In Cain's engagement with sin, it is sin that has the upper hand. Sin is the stronger party. Its desire is not fawning. It is an attitude of manipulation, a way of entrapping Cain and of subjecting him to its designs. If we allow this resonance to sound in the previous passage, too, the one in which God addresses Eve, the tables are turned. The woundedness of male–female relations after the fall is not a matter of one being fatally at the mercy of the other; it is a matter of each attempting to exploit and control the other, albeit by different means. Communion has given way to rivalry and menace: such are the wages of sin. This is where healing is required by grace and patient effort both between men and women and within each one of us, in so far as there, too, there is strife of this kind to be reconciled.

Håkan Hagegård as Papageno in Ingmar Bergman's television production from 1974, flanked by Irma Urrila's Pamina. Together the two characters sing, '[Love's] high purpose is evident: nothing is nobler than to tend, as woman and man, man and woman, woman and man, towards divinity.' Bergman had a profound understanding of the opera. He insisted that it is 'no silly fairytale' and spoke of 'the gospel of the Magic Flute'.

ORDER AND DISORDER

Catholic moral theology qualifies certain inclinations and types of behaviour as being 'objectively disordered'. It may appear a harsh-sounding phrase. In normal speech, to be 'disordered' is to be wrongly put together. Who can presume to make that kind of judgement of another? In theology, meanwhile, the language of 'order' and 'disorder' has a different resonance. We shall need to do some groundwork to hear these words truly, as the Church intends them.

A good place to begin is the Septuagint's rendering of Genesis 2.1, telling of God's outlook over creation on the seventh day: καὶ συνετελέσθησαν ὁ οὐρανὸς καὶ ἡ γῆ καὶ πᾶς ὁ κόσμος αὐτῶν. Jerome put this into Latin as, '*Igitur perfecti sunt caeli et terra, et omnis ornatus eorum*', which produced the now charmingly quaint-sounding version of the Douay-Rheims Bible: 'So the heavens and the earth were finished, and all the furniture of them.' What on the first day had been 'void and empty' (Genesis 1.2) is fully furnished. The Vulgate translates the Greek κόσμος (*kosmos*) as '*ornatus*'. Ornateness is tantamount to beauty, but beauty that springs, not from a random heaping-up of lovely things; this beauty is produced by the perfectly thought-out coherence of the whole. The root sense of '*kosmos*' is 'order'. We still draw on this sense in certain circumstances. The function of cosmetics is subtly to accentuate a facial symmetry that, unaided, might escape our notice.

At the beginning, human nature was perfectly part of this perfect order. It was oriented towards eternal life and the manifestation of God's substantial grace. Man and woman, creatures of dust, were robed in glory, called to carry transcendence into creation and to live in a tension uniting earth and heaven, the material and spiritual realms, not only in their souls and minds, but in their bodies. Their very existence had a unifying, priestly character. 'Like a priest with fragrant incense', wrote St Ephrem, 'Adam's keeping of the commandment was to be his censer.' The commandment carried into the moral and rational order the existential imperative of configuring man's iconic potential – his being created in God's image – to God's *likeness*. Man was invited to choose beatitude, which meant he was at liberty to reject it. His sacerdotal sacrifice lay in the ordering of his free will according to God's call.

Man's decision to disobey, to direct himself by appetite rather than by trust in God's precept, disrupted this order. The event we refer to as the 'fall' represents a corporate descent into disorder, a reality you and I, postlapsarians, take for granted: we have known nothing else.

St Paul provides an analytical summary of the drama which Genesis 3 relates by way of narrative. This is how he goes about it in Romans 5.12-19, which I have conflated in order to demonstrate the principal theses that interest us.

> Sin came into the world through one man, and death through sin, and so death spread to all because all have sinned. Death reigned from Adam to Moses, even over those whose sins were not like the transgression of Adam, who was a type of the one who was to come. For as by one man's disobedience many were made sinners, so by the one man's obedience many will be made righteous.

Paul traces a chain of causes and effects that upset original *kosmos*. This chain sets out from *disobedience*, a perversion of the will causing man to choose a course whose nefarious consequence is known to him: God had stated that, were he not to keep the (one and only) commandment set for him in Eden, he would die (Genesis 2.17).

Adam's disobedience is described by Paul as *trespass* or *transgression*. These English terms well convey the sense of their Greek equivalents παράπτωμα (*paraptōma*, from *piptō*, meaning 'to fall') and παράβασις (*parabasis*, from *bainō*, meaning 'to go'). They are concrete nouns to do with movement. The first syllable of 'tres-pass' contracts the 'trans' we find in 'transgression'. The Latin preposition 'trans' corresponds to the Greek 'para' – think of 'paranormal', which refers to phenomena beside or beyond a norm which they subvert. So *parabasis* means an 'overstepping', *paraptōma* a 'falling beside'. A direct path had been pointed out to Adam to take him on a straight, joyful journey through life, from time into eternity without interruption, enabling him, the royal priest, to rise to full stature as a son of God by adoption. He willingly rejected this itinerary. He chose instead to fall into a ditch, then to roll into the bushes, where we find him, who had stood, a moment ago, unselfconsciously dignified at the heart of creation, hiding for shame 'among the trees', seeking to avoid both the face of God and the gaze of his fellow human creature (Genesis 3.8).

This state of affairs, says Paul, can be generically labelled as *sin*. Here, too, we are dealing with a word whose history is rich in lessons. The New Testament word for 'sin', ἁμαρτία (*hamartia*), is derived from a verb that, in ancient Greek, was used of games. It meant 'to miss the mark' in the javelin or in archery. Later it came to denote, more generally, 'to fail of one's purpose'. So used are we to thinking of sin in terms of *guilt* that it is useful to be attuned to this semantic range. Sin, which conditions us all, is of its nature disordering, attracting us away from the goal towards which we would naturally move, had our nature not been struck with a cognitive affliction. To live in this state of bewilderment, says Paul (and this is the fourth, last element in his causal chain), is *death*, the opposite of the thriving for which we were made, which is not just a state of animation, but glorious, transformative fullness of being in God.

It should be clear that, on this reading, we all live lives marked by disorder, be it simply for the fact that we live with the prospect of death, an anomaly in the *kosmos* God intended. Whatever diverts us from the realization of personhood in communion with others, from the healing of the rift between man and woman, from the choice of generative life and the rejection of a culture of death, from the divinization by grace of our humanity – all this is, formally speaking, disordering, pulling us away, be it pleasurably, from our God-given purpose, potentially causing us to set off into the wilderness instead of finding our way to the Vision of Peace, the New Jerusalem 'compact together' (cf. Psalm 121.3), where the promise made in Eden is fulfilled and our nature perfected, with that in us which is of the image of God perfectly conformed to him who *is* the Image, our peace and delight for eternity.

Presupposing this background, the *Catechism of the Catholic Church* thus speaks, for example, of the disordered exploitation of natural goods harming the environment (n. 339), of a disordered attachment to creatures causing forgetfulness of the Creator (n. 1394), of lying and calumny, the trampling underfoot of truth, as being 'intrinsically disordered' behaviour (n. 1753), of a 'disordered desire for money' disrupting the social order (n. 2424), and so forth. In all these instances we see a possible good diverted from its true finality. Disorder stands for a re-emergence of something of that primeval chaos over which the Spirit hovered to produce from elemental forces that which was, is, and forever remains good.

Disorder can make itself felt, too, in the intimacy of our hearts, bodies and relationships. The *Catechism* speaks of disordered appetites (n. 37). These make themselves felt as lust – '*luxuria*' in the Latin typical edition. *Luxuria* contrasts with healthy desire in as much as it is not directed towards communion, through surrender with another, but intent on self-satisfaction, for which purpose another human being is instrumentalized, not encountered as a person, but used as a means towards an end. Lust is thus 'disordered desire for or inordinate enjoyment of sexual pleasure', and sexual pleasure is 'morally disordered when sought for itself, isolated from its procreative and unitive purposes' (n. 2351).

We face a near-universal problem. Rare are those men and women who have never found sexual desire, in itself noble, to be overwhelming and confused. We are vulnerable in this area. The core of our physical being is touched. We are susceptible to being terribly hurt, apt to hurt terribly. To submit that we will benefit, and benefit others, by learning self-ordering is simply to appeal to experience: it is what Kamala taught Siddhartha, who had come to her to learn the art of love.

In a perspective of faith, the stakes are higher. The believer knows that the senses ultimately yearn for ecstasy beyond the sensual. Deep calls on deep at the noise of floodgates that contain, in frail flesh, energies which are of God and rise towards God (cf. Psalm 41.8). We are carried to the limit of creaturehood.

A verse from the Song of Songs frequently recurs in the writings of the Cistercian Fathers: '*Ordinavit in me caritatem*,' 'You have set love in order in me' (Song of Songs 2.4, according to the Vulgate). The Fathers took it for granted that all men would need such ordering. A century or so later a school of remarkable Cistercian nuns, based at Helfta, explored what such ordering might mean from a feminine perspective. These men and women were mystically minded. But they were fully of flesh and blood. They shared this conviction: the fruitful ordering of human love can only be fully accomplished when the ordering principle is Wisdom from above. Here we might recall Claudel's observation that Wisdom's Scriptural form is feminine. 'O Sapientia', the Church sings on 17 December, when it enters the last, luminous phase of Advent:

> O Sapientia, quae ex ore Altissimi prodisti, attingens a fine usque ad finem fortiter suaviterque disponens omnia: veni ad docendum nos viam prudentiae.

> O Wisdom, proceeding from the mouth of the Most High, reaching from one end to the other and ordering all things with strength and sweetness: come and teach us the way of prudence.

Have we always expounded the Church's teaching on the ordering of affection in a way that matches the strength of our words with corresponding sweetness? Sometimes, perhaps on account of inexperience, we may have wanted for prudence, making a loveable goal, gloriously vindicated through the incarnation, appear as little other than a bleak mid-winter freezing of desire.

Delicacy is called for in the re-ordering of disordered love. We are dealing not with programmable machines, but with embodied souls, than which nothing in creation is more sensitive. To channel this sensitivity is a demanding proposition. In a conversation with Bruno Monsaingeon in 1994 Yehudi Menuhin, speaking of himself as a young man, declared that he had been 'very vindictive' and 'very, very passionate'. He added: 'I don't know what kind of character I would have been had I not been able to fulfil myself to a certain extent. I might have been a very unbalanced character . . . But anyway, all of that went into the music.' This is a statement of universal validity. You may object: I am not possessed of creative genius crying out for expression! That may be true. But we all carry in us, such is the Christian's conviction, a desire to be consecrated, for our being to be divinized. That amounts to a fantastic affective impetus, which can result in imbalance if not ordered well.

Much in a person's life can stand in the way of affection's right ordering. Privations and surfeits, wounds and attachments from early on can set lives on a path that goes against the ordered grain, an 'objectively disordered' path which nonetheless seems to the person concerned the only path possible, the only chance to find fulfilment and joy. Such situations call for respect and patience. To say this is not to call the *kosmos* into question. It is to regard the complexity of life with intelligent compassion in truth, a prerequisite for pastoral care and for friendship.

Further, things are often not quite what they seem. Apparent promiscuity may be a default way of dealing with a burden of love or anguish. Etty Hillesum wrote in her diary on 4 September 1941: 'I am unhappy again. I can quite see why people get drunk or go to bed with a total stranger.' So imperious can our need for consolation be. Etty realised, though, 'that isn't really my way.' What her way was she gradually learned. In November 1941, in a watershed moment, she knelt for the first time in her life, on her bathroom floor. In December she wrote, 'The foolish and passionate desire to "lose myself" in [Spier, her lover] has long ago vanished, has grown "sensible". All

I have left of that feeling is the will to "yield" myself to God, or to a poem.'

She did not stop reverencing human love; she dug to its core and discovered it to be a symbol pointing towards an encompassing reality. She wished for something absolute. A single destiny or passion was no longer enough for her. 'God', a word that had spelt for her an ideal notion, came to point towards a presence within reach. While in this movement of ascent, she saw at the same time that subsisting at high altitude is hard: 'I shall probably have to seek my deliverance in bad pieces of prose,' she noted, before wryly adding, 'just as a man *in extremis* may seek deliverance in what is aptly called a "tart", because he needs someone to still his deep hunger.'

As the months passed, she came to probe this hunger ever more deeply. Etty Hillesum set off to Westerbork in 1943 carrying her New Testament and Rilke's letters, faithful to her intent, expressed on 29 May 1942, to 'look things straight in the face, even the worst crimes, and to discover the small, naked human being amid the monstrous wreckage caused by man's senseless deeds'. The chronicle of her determination recounts a life that is little by little transfigured in charity.

Etty's was in many ways an objectively disordered itinerary, not without trespasses, which she readily acknowledged; yet a pattern of order was secretly being formed by the strangely coloured threads that composed her life's tapestry in patterns that, seen from too close up, seemed simply deranged.

Jacques Lusseyran touches on a similar paradox when he speaks of the fifteen months he spent in Buchenwald until his release on 12 April 1945. That period taught him a great deal about human nature. He saw men who, in ordinary life, had been ordering pillars of society: in the camp they rose at night to steal others' bread. He saw believers 'who sought their faith everywhere, yet did not find it, or found it was so small it was no use to them' in an environment void of pious props. What astonished him, though, was the goodness he found in unexpected places:

> How do you explain that in Block 56, my block, the one person to volunteer day and night for months to look after the furiously insane, calming them and feeding them, to care for those suffering from cancer, dysentery and typhoid, to wash and comfort them, was a man who, so everyone said, was in civil life an effete *salon* pederast, one of those men in whose company one would not like to be seen. Yet here he was, the good angel – no, we must say more: the saint, the only saint, of the infirmary block.

The love in us that needs to be ordered is not just of the carnal kind. It can happen that disorder in the realm of physical passion coexists with order – with 'the beauty of order', as people liked to say in the Middle Ages – in the higher sphere of charity. God, who sees everything from on high, will evaluate as a whole these parallel processes unfolding bewilderingly within the confines of a single life.

The way to order, for most of us, goes *through* disorder; to try to sidestep it is to risk sidestepping life. To be aware, be it subliminally, of the disorder I carry, yet to pretend it does not exist, is to entertain illusion. On that basis no meaningful relationship, and no spiritual life, is possible. How can I ever be healed if I am determined to give the impression I am not sick?

'I have come', declares the Lord, 'not to call the righteous but sinners to conversion' (Luke 5.32). If you admit the definitions proposed at the beginning of this section, we might paraphrase: 'I have not come to call those who in any case walk straight (for they know where they are going); my mission is to those who have taken a wrong turn. I call them by proposing *metanoia*, a new outlook on reality.' Christ, 'the fairest of the sons of men' (Psalm 44.2), reveals order's beauty. But he is not surprised by our disorder, however shabby it may be.

When we read the lives of saints, we repeatedly see God's magnanimity in letting men and women act out lengthy spells of disorder preceding their awakening to grace, as if the seven days of creation, with gradual distinctions, were re-enacted in individual lives; as if we all had to make a customized exodus journey home from Egypt – not such a long trip, really, but protracted by serial rebellions, delays and misapprehensions. These, too, play their part in God's providence. They are meant to teach us something: 'You shall remember all the way which the Lord your God has led you these forty years in the wilderness, that he might humble you, testing you to know what was in your heart, whether you would keep his commandments, or not' (Deuteronomy 8.2). This remains the bottom line when it comes to confronting *my* disorder. Am I prepared to own and name that which is in my heart? Will I, from that point of departure, let God's call order and reform me?

Yehudi Menuhin at 12, in 1928. In old age he said about this stage of
his life: 'As a small child, I imagined that if I could play the Chaconne
of Bach inspiringly enough in the Sistine Chapel, under the eyes of
Michelangelo, all that is ignoble and vile would miraculously disappear
from our world.' To entertain such thoughts so early in life is sublime
and terrifying. What tension within! Tension that must somehow be
ordered and released so as not to implode destructively.

Eros and Death

The Second Book of Samuel tells the story of a very public adultery. The story begins with the words, 'It happened, late one afternoon, when David arose from his couch and was walking upon the roof of the king's house, that he saw from the roof a woman bathing; and the woman was very beautiful' (2 Samuel 11.2). The king was aroused. He called for the woman, slept with her, and sent her away, treating her as a harlot, though no mention is made of an emolument. When the woman, Bathsheba, later sent word that she had conceived, David's concern was to conceal his agency.

He had Bathsheba's husband Uriah, a royal officer, recalled from the war he was fighting under David's banner, hoping he would use home leave to spend a pleasant night at home. Uriah, a conscientious fellow, declined. He told David, 'The Ark and Israel and Judah dwell in booths; and my lord Joab and the servants of my lord are camping in the open field; shall I then go to my house, to eat and to drink, and to lie with my wife?' (2 Samuel 11.11). At this David coolly adopted a different approach. He had Uriah re-despatched to the front and assigned to a position in which death in battle was assured. Why? To keep himself from losing face, to avoid having to confront a subaltern and admit that he, the Lord's Anointed, had casually trodden both on a divine commandment and on the law of common decency.

It is an extraordinary feature of the Hebrew Bible that it recounts so matter-of-factly the abysmal moral failure of one of its heroes. Proposing the perfectibility of human nature, Scripture insists that it is wholly God's work. Left to our devices we are capable of falling to great depths. David's adultery was not a momentary surrender to disorder in the heat of passion; it was calculated and violent. The king did not think twice of assassinating Uriah and, alongside him, other faithful soldiers; the manoeuvre by which he had Bathsheba's husband done away with was suicidal, strategically speaking. The whole battalion suffered loss (11.16-21). When report was made to David, he sent to tell Joab, the commander, 'Do not let this matter trouble you' (11.25). It is unsettling to find, in Holy Writ, a statement that would not sound out of place in the drawl of Marlon Brando's Godfather. Such is the power of blinded *eros*. It can draw us into collusion with death.

David's action had consequences for his house and family. The thing he had done 'displeased the Lord' (11.27), who sent Nathan the prophet to chastise him and to say that as a result of his action, 'the sword shall never depart from your house' (12.10). Having sown the wind, he would reap the whirlwind (cf. Hosea 8.7). A curse did fall thenceforth on David's house. Shortly after the murder of Uriah, David's son Amnon committed incest with his half-sister Tamar. Obsessed by the thought of her, he summoned her, ravished her, then spurned her, finding that, as soon as his fantasy was spent, he felt for her nothing but disdain, 'indeed, his loathing was even greater than the lust he had felt for her' (13.15).

Absalom, another of David's sons, learned what had happened. He avenged his sister Tamar by murdering Amnon, his brother, falling into a morbid pattern: the first recorded death in human history, as Scripture recounts it, was a death by fratricide (Genesis 4.8). The son whom David begot by Bathsheba once the child born of their first union had died, was Solomon. His career was stellar, yet there runs throughout it a sinister undercurrent, linked with lust. 'Solomon loved many foreign women . . .

Among his wives were 700 princesses and 300 concubines' (1 Kings 11.1-3). Allowing for rhetorical hyperbole the picture painted is one of institutionalized compulsion. Surrender to self-obsessed *eros* dulled Solomon's spiritual senses: 'his wives turned away his heart after other gods; and his heart was not true to the Lord his God' (11.4). To enthrone lust as the heart's governor is to surrender to idolatry. As a result (11.11), the bond between the land and the Davidic line was severed. After Solomon's death the kingdom was divided. National integrity would be for millennia but a fond memory.

It gives food for thought that the inspired authors trace this rot, affecting a whole people, back to a particular act of death-dealing *luxuria*.

David's act and its impact are imprinted on Christian consciousness. A key text in liturgical prayer is Psalm 50, 'A Psalm', says the Septuagint, 'of David, when Nathan the Prophet went to him, after he had gone in to Bathsheba'. We tend to dismiss these narrative headings nowadays, considering that modern research has given us a more sophisticated view of the Psalter. What interests us is not the construct of Davidic romance, but the possibility of detecting Ugaritic antecedents.

Yet there is nothing naïve about the Davidization of the Psalter. Athanasius says, in his *Letter to Marcellinus*, that the Psalter contains all of Scripture by abbreviation, as if in an enclosed garden (n. 2). The believer is to make this garden his own, to walk the length and breadth of it, finding there authoritative articulation of 'the movements of each individual soul, the ways in which it changes and the means it needs to correct itself' (n. 12). The attribution of this panorama to David makes him like Everyman in medieval drama. He represents the human condition.

Finding David in the Psalms, I find myself in them. They reveal me to myself.

For it is not only we who read the Psalter. The Psalter reads us. It is like 'a mirror to the one who prays, letting him contemplate himself and the movements of his soul in them' (n. 12) – and by no means only the edifying movements. The Psalter confronts us with our heart's darkness. Have we the nerve to enter it, it can have a cathartic effect, like the performance of tragic drama. That is why the censoring of the Psalter for liturgical use, pruning it of passages we deem not nice, is misconceived. It makes of the Psalter a book of devotions rather than, as Athanasius taught, the measure of 'the whole of human existence' (n. 30).

St Benedict ordained that monks, seekers after truth, should sing Psalm 50 each day at dawn. Every time the sun rises they are to remember King David in disgrace, and so be mindful of that in themselves which resists grace, while imploring the Lord to pardon, order and heal. There is timeless immediacy in this text, whether it is recited monodically in a monastic choir, solemnly performed (the way Mozart at 14 heard it in Allegri's setting), or murmured solitarily, as in the introspective paraphrase of Thomas Wyatt, a poet who, in his dealings with Henry VIII, did not lack occasion to meditate on the misdemeanours of princes:

And I beknow my fault, my negligence,
And in my sight my sin is fixed fast,
Thereof to have more perfect penitence.
To thee alone, to thee have I trespassed
For none can measure my fault but thou alone.
For in thy sight I have not been aghast

For to offend, judging thy sight as none
So that my fault were hid from sight of man,
Thy majesty so far from my mind was gone.

Note Wyatt's stress on retreat from visibility to hiddenness, from lucidity to fantasy. *Eros*, says one of our times' best authorities on this matter, stands for 'a kind of intoxication, the overpowering of reason by a "divine madness" which tears man away from his finite existence and enables him to experience supreme happiness'. Ordered clear-sightedly it can give a foretaste 'of the pinnacle of our existence, of that beatitude for which our whole being yearns'. Left to ache blindly, it becomes 'warped and destructive'. An absolutization of *eros* 'strips it of its dignity and dehumanizes it'. Blind *eros*, claiming omnipotence, imprisons us in ourselves, closing our eyes to the other instead of opening our eyes. Let us consider three aspects of the dynamic by which this vital force can turn death-dealing.

We may call the first aspect erotic intoxication. In such cases *eros* is conceived of as a force of agency that elevates human beings in an ecstasy pushing at life's extremity. We have an account of it in Wagner's opera *Tristan and Isolde*. This work, premiered at Ludwig of Bavaria's Königliches Hoftheater in 1865, was inspired by a twelfth-century romance, but its mood is Wagnerian through and through. The opera posits the relatedness of *eros* to death, which Siddhartha discovered in Kamala's school. The two are figured in two magic potions, one of extinction, the other of love.

Act One shows us the Irish princess Isolde aboard a ship, on her way to an arranged marriage in Cornwall. She is consumed with rage and sadness. Her future husband's agent, Tristan, once slew her heart's true love. Isolde might have killed Tristan then, but did not; now, facing a future she abhors, she would repair past negligence. She asks her maid to prepare a mortal potion she intends to drink with Tristan to finish off both him and herself. The maid, changing the recipe, mixes a love potion instead. As soon as Tristan and Isolde drink it, the world about them – the wind, the sun, the salty sea – ceases to exist. They have eyes for nothing but each other. They do not meet each other's gaze. They drown in it, telling each other, 'You are me, I am you, I am no longer myself.' Their chemically induced passion cancels any meaningful notion of 'self'. Mooring at Cornwall, Tristan exclaims,

O Wonne voller Tücke! O truggeweihtes Glücke!

O wileful bliss! O happiness pledged to deceit!

He is unselved by what lives in him. He knows that this is so, yet surrenders. Isolde does the same. The sweetness of annihilating bliss is too great.

When the two reunite in Act Two, their euphoric singing leaves us in no doubt: they are quite out of their minds. Later in the same act, wileful bliss reveals its true face as perversion, spelt out in Wagner's libretto. The music is gorgeous. The words are lovely, too. Charmed, we must really pay attention to note the sickness of erotic inebriation in which there is no trace of romance. Tristan and Isolde seek, not communion, but possession. Possession, they see, can only become final in death. They start to yearn for death. Renouncing the day, they opt for the night. Their choice contrasts with a key New Testament motif: 'We are not of the night, nor of darkness' (1 Thessalonians 5.5). In a spiralling duet they sing:

O sink hernieder,	Descend
Nacht der Liebe,	O Night of Love,
gib Vergessen,	grant forgetfulness
dass ich lebe;	that I may live;
nimm mich auf	take me up
in deinen Schoss,	into your bosom,
löse von	release me
der Welt mich los!	from the world.

The *Liebestod* motif makes its first appearance in an effusion of Tristan's, aspiring to be 'ever one' with Isolde, yet to be 'nameless', deprived of personhood, offered up to a divinized Love which uncannily resembles ancient Moloch, who consumed his children. When Isolde develops the theme at the end of the opera, the music's sublimity, cutting right through us, can make us forget that she is, in fact, throwing herself dying into the arms of a corpse. Such is the fulfilment of this kind of *eros*.

The German director Christoph Schlingensief, adulated for his productions of Wagner, reflected on this theme in a 2009 memoir subtitled 'A Diary of Illness by Cancer'. The cancer in question claimed his life the following year. 'I am sure,' he wrote, 'that in my case cancer is somehow linked to Bayreuth'. He says he has come to believe that Wagner's music is 'dangerous music, celebrating not life, but death'. Immersion in this imaginative world had led him 'to open a door within myself I ought never to have opened'. He does not blame Wagner. But he maintains that the *eros* immortalized by Wagner can lead into, precisely, a night in which there is no light by which to move. He cites the conductor

Christian Thielemann as saying, 'I'll never conduct *Tristan* again. It is the death of one.' Schlingensief adds, 'Quite'. The divinization of *eros* is not innocent. Even false gods require offerings.

The grand Shakespearean actress Gwen Ffrangcon-Davies hints at like awareness in an interview she gave in 1988, aged ninety seven. Clearly still moved, she referred to what she called 'one of the greatest experiences of my whole life'.

> It was just after the war. I was staying with Ivor Novello, who was a very great friend of Kirsten Flagstad's. And she'd come over here to sing in a performance to raise money for the Save the Children Fund. It was in the Harringay Arena. She came trotting in, onto the arena; I can see her now, in a little flowered dress, bowing and smiling, and went up onto the stage and then sat. And the minute the music started, the first note – Malcolm Sargent was conducting –, she became . . . a dedicated priestess. And when she sang, it was . . . her voice . . . I can only describe it: it was molten gold.

Flagstad sang Isolde's *Liebestod*. Ffrangcon-Davies sat entranced, hand in hand with Sybil Thorndike: 'Tears were pouring down our faces.' The two felt they were being translated into a different realm. *Eros*, be it through high art, touches depths in us for which we have no words. It calls forth a sacrificial impulse of which we may not be aware – except in the darkness of the night. It matters to resolve freely in advance, in the light of day, at which altar we wish to perform it.

A second aspect of the *eros*–death nexus takes violent form, at least implicitly. Harold Pinter evokes it in the

opening dialogue of *Ashes to Ashes*, a play first presented
in London in 1996. It is an unsettling scene. There are
only two characters on stage, Devlin and Rebecca. When
the curtain parts we see 'Devlin standing with a drink.
Rebecca sitting'. There is silence. Then:

REBECCA
Well . . . for example . . . he would stand over me and
clench his fist. And then he'd put his other hand on my
neck and grip it and bring my head towards him. His
fist . . . grazed my mouth. And he'd say, 'Kiss my fist.'

DEVLIN
And did you?

REBECCA
Oh yes. I kissed his fist. The knuckles. And then he'd
open his hand and give me the palm of his hand . . . to
kiss . . . which I kissed.

Pause

And then I would speak.

DEVLIN
What did you say? You said what? What did you say?

Pause

REBECCA
I said, 'Put your hand round my throat.' I murmured it
through his hand, as I was kissing it, but he heard my
voice, he heard it through his hand, he felt my voice in
his hand, he heard it there.

Silence

DEVLIN
And did he? Did he put his hand round your throat?

REBECCA
Oh yes. He did. He did. And he held it there, very
gently, very gently, so gently. He adored me, you see.

The identity of the man from Rebecca's past remains
unclear in the play. So does the precise nature of their
relationship, even as the unknown man's posture and
gestures are gradually, sinisterly adopted by Devlin, who
initially purported to deplore them. A few contextual clues
are given, images suggestive of Holocaust movies, but we
must look outside the text for a *Sitz im Leben*. We find
it, of all places, in an essay by Gitta Sereny, the intrepid
historian of Nazism and biographer of Albert Speer.

In 1998 an actor friend told Sereny that Pinter had
written the play 'after reading your book'. The playwright
confirmed this, saying he was intrigued by the paradox
Speer embodied. While masterminding Hitler's slave-
labour factories, Speer remained 'a very civilized man . . .
horrified by what he saw when he visited the factories'. He
was outwardly humane, yet ruthless. He inspired affection
while facilitating violence. This sets the scene for *Ashes to
Ashes*, a play that, according to Sereny, is 'about a man and
a woman who both care for and hate one another, and
explores the way in which force and coercion can produce
sexual magnetism'.

As if through a magnifying glass it shows us the worst
of the conflict between Adam and Eve after the fall, albeit
in the setting of an English drawing room.

The scene Pinter puts before us is one we would, frankly, rather not consider. The imposition of male force is troubling. Even more so is Rebecca's submission and her affirmation, 'He adored me, you see.' Her statement takes us to the heart of the matter. Human beings sometimes rationalize humiliation and hurt in terms of desire. It can seem a way of holding on to influence or agency in the midst of affective obliteration. When such recourse is channelled through physical instinct, it can present itself erotically, even though the realization of *eros* entails compulsive repetition of past pain. Two individuals can be locked in a mutually destructive dynamic: one acting out a claim to omnipotence; the other melting into compliance, fantastically construed as a state of being desired and valued.

Liliana Cavani brought a representation of this psychological complex to celluloid in 1974 with her film *The Night Porter*. In it, a former concentration camp guard meets an ex-prisoner in a smart Viennese hotel after the war. Ostensibly their roles have been reversed: he is a mere porter, she a wealthy guest. They are inexorably drawn back, though, into their relation as it formerly was, defined by dominance on his part, servility on hers. The film sparked controversy. Vincent Canby began a fulgurating review in the *New York Times* with, 'Let us now consider a piece of junk.' An argument can be made for a more tempered approach.

Cavani's script came out of in-depth conversations with female camp survivors. She was struck by the need many had to return to places in which they had suffered degradation. Their goal was not just to remember what had happened, but to keep confronting a part of themselves. One said, 'I shall never forgive the Nazis for having made me touch a part of myself I did not know was there.' We can go to great lengths to survive, to find comfort, to make sense to ourselves of what *is* senseless. That is how we try to hang on to a dream of dignity.

'Our nature', says Cavani, 'is complex, sometimes a lot more complex than we think.' It is no coincidence that both she and Pinter chose the backdrop of World War Two to conduct enquiries into fatal *eros*. The universe of the camps is a symbolic touchstone for Western consciousness. By it, we distinguish darkness from light – at least we have done so for the past seventy years, while the Shoah has been kept in corporate remembrance: the scandal of amnesia lies before us now.

Against this backdrop, evil is relatively easy to pinpoint. The risk is that we think perverse behaviour confined to extreme environments. We have been poorly prepared to acknowledge it in our midst, not to mention in environments supposed to be radiant with light.

The unravelling of abuse in the Church has been terrible. It has forced us to diagnose an ulcerating wound in need of healing. We face a legacy of sin and crime that calls out for reparation. We recognize patterns of abusive behaviour. Thereby, and this is an advantage, we are helped to develop effective measures of prevention. A key insight gained pertains to the link between sexual abuse and the abuse of power. Such abuse is often minutely calculated. Pinter's and Cavani's scenarios find their counterpart in testimonies about clerical abuse now available, alas, in abundance.

We see seduction used to construct a web in which a victim is trapped, bound by spiritual dependence and loyalty, even the sense of being 'adored'. We hear of instances of Christ's name being blasphemously used as a tool of power to establish a grip on another's life every bit as tight as the one that introduces *Ashes to Ashes*.

At the outset there may have been grace, or what felt like it. The testimony of one former nun begins with words addressed to her confessor, who later abused her: 'I was sixteen when I met you. Without you I doubt I'd ever have risen from the state I was in, wrecked by pain, cast up onto childhood's riverbed. The light you carried restored meaning to my life.' Yet within this context of light, unfreedom encroached. The young girl was flattered by the priest's claim to see in her a born contemplative. 'Will you let me guide you?' he asked. How could she not? Did he not embody mystic power? Guidance would require, she was told, surrender on her part. The form which that surrender took over time is spelled out. 'He held between his hands my brain, my heart, my soul, my spirit, and my body.' When she protested that it could not be right for him to move her hands underneath his habit, she was told, 'It is a gift of God. At this degree of love, the two have but one desire.' Then: 'I owe the fruitfulness of my apostolate to our relationship.' She must cast aside scruples, he insisted. Did he not offer Mass after their trysts? Did that not prove that what took place between them was blessed? Erotic coercion is exercised, in this example, by means of words and charisma. Nonetheless, its violence is deadly.

The third tendency I wish to signal under this heading is pornographic. Pornographic *eros* is unilateral. It has no encounter in view, only self-indulgence. Rooted in a consumerist mindset, it slots easily into the logic by which our society works. In a world of free trade, it somehow seems reasonable to purchase stimuli by which to still – at least momentarily – sensual appetite. The explosion of pornographic trade shows how widely this mindset is adopted. The trade's managers vindicate it in terms of consumers' 'freedom' to desire. The flip side is the epidemic spread of pornographic addiction, a servitude as cruel as any.

Auto-eroticism considers only one subject-agent. The lust object is regarded precisely as such, an *object* deprived of personhood, a physical presence whose function, and sole interest, is to satisfy another's desire. We have considered the significance of *prosōpon*, the Greek word for 'person'. In antiquity, a negated form of this noun was used as a synonym for 'slave': *aprosōpon*, literally, 'a faceless one', an identityless human form become merchandise. The term is of obvious relevance to performers of pornographic make-believe. Their faces are not what viewers look for.

But what if such an *aprosōpon* reveals a human face? What if a voiceless one begins to speak? The chances are we shall find bottomless sorrow.

Such sorrow is put into words in the harrowing autobiography of Somaly Mam, a Cambodian woman first raped at twelve, then, at fifteen, given to a soldier in marriage as payment for debt, then sold into prostitution. From infancy she was regarded as 'money on legs, an asset, a kind of domestic livestock'. Her husband was savage: 'Many soldiers are.' We sense the wounds he carried, results of terrible things seen and done. This does not excuse him. But it shows how vulnerability may transmute into violence, in a lethal spiral.

During her first years in the brothel, Somaly Mam remained in a state of rebellion. She loathed what she had become, being bought and sold, subjected to humiliations and excruciating pain. Repeatedly she tried to run away. Each time she got caught. 'I tried never to look a client in the eye,' she writes. She did not want to see the reflection of what he saw when he looked at her. It was a minimal but conscious act of defiance.

Gradually, she had no more strength to defy. She came to think that her fate was sealed. Of all the heart-wrenching aspects of her story, none perhaps is more tragic than the change that took place when she was not yet twenty: 'from that point on I capitulated.' The light in her eyes was gone. She accepted to see herself the way others saw her, as Nobody: 'I told myself I was dead.' She did not even have a name. When later she managed to establish a new life for herself, she adopted 'Somaly Mam', which means Lost in the Forest. 'It was the truest name.'

This story, too, is a story of extremes, yet it speaks of universals. It permits us to see how dehumanizing *eros* can become when indulged as the craving of a hungry subject consuming faceless others as fodder, whether in the flesh or virtually.

This kind of *eros* is in the strict sense *perverted*, that is, 'turned away' from its purpose. Instead of creating communion, it accentuates loneliness. The chances are that it also arises from loneliness. That is why it must be dealt with sensitively.

Men can find it difficult to recognize this aspect of sexuality. Perhaps too much of their self-image is at stake. Women often see it with greater precision, even compassion. A pathetic picture of the genesis of potentially perverted *eros* is painted by Jennifer Lash in her novel *Blood Ties*, the story of a dysfunctional family.

We follow one character from conception. He is called Spencer, named after the Fulham pub the Spencer Arms. Spencer is the fruit of a union between the elusive Lumsden and Dolly, a nineteen-year-old child unfit to be a mother. 'Spencer, born on a day of considerable cold in mid-winter in England, was one among millions. At first unnamed, he struggled for warmth, response and nourishment like all the rest.' These he failed to find. His mother 'was fearful to get to know him'.

> Every close contact with him when they were alone seemed to leach her; his very touch, the weight of him if he fell against her, the scramble of him trying to get on to her knee or into her bed, seemed to threaten her, to accost her. She would push him back with increasing ferocity. When simply his presence became too much for her, she would keep him shut up in the small bedroom, while she sat alone biting her nails and smoking cigarettes in front of the flickering black-and-white television screen.

It is senseless to intrude into such melancholy with facile attributions of guilt. Poor Dolly could not give what she had not. That did not keep her indigence from having a defining impact on Spencer. Meeting no response outside, seeing no one look at him, the child turned in on himself. He cried less often, for what was the use of it? He refused to eat. 'The extent of his self-expression was denial, refusal, silence.'

Something strange happened to his eyes. It was remarked on by Lily, a friend of Dolly's.

> 'Those fish eyes', Lily said, 'they'd haunt me. They're not the eyes of a child, no way.' But of course they were the eyes of a child. But a child who had to find some manner to contain within himself, within his small limbs and frail person, the stench, the refuse of

all the attempts he had made to extend, to proceed, to find, which had always been instantly rebuffed and returned to him. Unable to receive, he would stagnate; he would stagnate with all the experience, the sight and sounds and sense he could not give, buried into the little, dump housing of himself . . . More and more the things which engaged him had to be anything over which he had both access and control.

He was an infant. That something could only be his body. Lash, mother of seven, writes with pity of the one way Spencer had of affirming to himself that he was alive. Having been whisked off to Ireland to Lumsden's frigid parents, to whom his arrival was 'most unsavoury and inconvenient', he finds himself for the first time in his life immersed in silence. It is not a beneficial, healing silence. It hangs over him 'like a fluttering bird, wings spread to the furthest emptiness'.

In a strange bed, in the high room, unslept in for so long, the weight of the silence was a brutal force, a huge constraint, a quiet, choking scheme without pattern or movement. Spencer kicked off the covers to make some space; to feel some sense on the rough skin of his legs and knees. He held his hand fast on the only sense agent still in his possession, he clung and wrung and rubbed his penis as if this movement could keep out the last final stiffness, that the weight of the bird and its stretched wings everywhere could reduce him to.

We might think his future prefigured in this nocturnal vision, with sexual gratification increasingly internalized as the one known means to pacify a legitimate and in itself healthy affective need. But no. Spencer turns out to exemplify man's capacity to conquer freedom against all odds. His yoke of loneliness is set to be shattered.

There is a warning, though, in this narrative, a reminder of the despair from which self-enclosed eroticism can spring and to which it can lead.

The ways in which *eros* is brushed by death's wing invite us to look into our hearts, asking God for truth there, and spaciousness, and openness to love. 'Then', as David sang once he realized what he had *done* to Bathsheba, owning his waywardness, 'shall for joy upspring/The bones that were afore consumed to dust' (from Psalm 50, again in Wyatt's version).

The Norwegian soprano Kirsten Flagstad (1895–1962) was proverbially fond of knitting. Here she is before her debut at Covent Garden in 1936, about to sing Isolde. If underneath this peaceful, matronly exterior a priestess to Eros could lie hidden, ready to surface when summoned, similar depths are likely to be found within all of us.

Marriage and Virginity

Towards the end of Deuteronomy, we find this provision about military service: 'When a man is newly married, he shall not go out with the army or be charged with any business; he shall be free at home one year, to rejoice with his wife whom he has taken' (24.5). The passage indicates the regard in which marriage was held in Biblical Israel, not just as a civic institution, but as an eruption of joy in the community. Scripture adopts the simile of marriage to describe God's relationship with his people, notably in Hosea, a book that makes it clear, at the same time, that the married state is no doddle. The joy of spouses is exacting. But what true joy is not?

In post-exilic Judaism the custom developed of greeting the sabbath in terms of nuptial rejoicing. 'Already in Talmudic time', notes Jonathan Sacks,

> Shabbat was seen as a bride, and the day itself as a wedding. 'Rabbi Chanina robed himself and stood on the eve of Shabbat at sunset and said, "Come, let us go and welcome Shabbat the queen." Rabbi Yannai donned his robes and said, "Come O Bride, come O Bride."'

This motif underlies a splendid hymn set for the conclusion of the candle-lighting rite that introduces the domestic service welcoming Shabbat. It was written by Rabbi Shlomo Alkabetz, Thomas Wyatt's senior by three years, who taught in Hadrianopolis. Each of the nine stanzas is followed by the refrain,

לְכָה דוֹדִי לִקְרַאת כַּלָּה פְּנֵי שַׁבָּת נְקַבְּלָה

Come, my Beloved, to greet the Bride; let us welcome
the Sabbath.

The final stanza reads,

בּוֹאִי בְשָׁלוֹם עֲטֶרֶת בַּעְלָהּ
גַּם בְּשִׂמְחָה וּבְצָהֳלָה
תּוֹ אֱמוּנֵי עַם סְגֻלָּה
בּוֹאִי כַלָּה בּוֹאִי כַלָּה

Come in peace, Crown of her husband;
Come with joy and jubilation,
Among the faithful of the treasured people.
Enter, O Bride! Enter, O Bride!

The image of the crown recalls a line from Proverbs, 'A good
wife is the crown of her husband' (12.4). There is resonance,
too, of the line from Psalm 8 we considered in Chapter Two:
'with glory and honour you crowned him' (Psalm 8.6). The
theological use of bridal imagery presupposes rootedness
in human reality. The emblem of the first dispensation of
grace, the crown, is restored to man by woman. By virtue
of their committed union, wholeness is given back to both.

This motif is enacted in the service of crowning
that remains an integral part of a Byzantine Christian
wedding. Having entered the church after exchanging
rings in the narthex, the bridal couple is questioned
by the priest as to the freedom of their commitment.
Prayers are said. The Great Litany is sung. The priest
then places a crown, first on the bridegroom's head,
then on the bride's, crowning each 'unto' the other. He
blesses the pair thrice, saying each time, 'O Lord our
God, crown them with glory and honour.' Does this

not indicate that, there and then, paradise is palpably
present on earth by way of a pledge? There is, in these
crowns, a reference to the crown of martyrdom. The
accompanying prayers make it explicit. The married state
is a state of Christian witness, ever costly. But above all
we behold the Edenic crown of glory, the restoration of
humankind to its primordial dignity.

It cannot be stressed enough that Christian marriage
is only comprehensible, and realizable, in the light of
this opening-up to transcendence. Christian marriage
is categorically distinct from a secular social contract. It
does not merely seal a bond between individuals who care
for one another. It enacts a re-creation, a fulfilment of
human nature in the healing of the wound of loneliness
inflicted by *sexus*, enabling woman and man to find
in one another the human completion for which each
yearns. Integration on the horizontal, relational plane
raises the two up, together, into a further communion
along a vertical axis. In the Byzantine marriage rite,
crowning is followed by a reading from the epistle of
St Paul to the Ephesians. It proclaims that the oneness
between husband and wife, while engaging them fully
in body, soul and mind, also points beyond them. It is
incarnate and concrete. At the same time it is iconic, the
symbol of a mystery: 'This mystery is a profound one,
and I am saying that it refers to Christ and the church'
(Ephesians 5.32).

No more radical way could be found of expressing
the reach of the bridal covenant. It foreshadows the
eschatological accomplishment of man's vocation for
whose sake, so the Fathers insisted, the world was made:
the final and eternal reconciliation of human and divine
nature envisaged in Scripture as the Marriage of the Lamb

(cf. Revelation 19.7). When this Marriage is accomplished, all flesh will cast their crowns before the throne of God in an act of adoration (cf. Revelation 4.10). There will be no further need for symbols when we are immersed in the real.

In the first centuries of Christianity, it was commonly assumed that the end of time was near, that our lovely but transient world would cease in whatever way it might please God to make this come about. What, then, was the point of marriage and procreation? Some denigrated the nuptial covenant as being earthbound, sexual intercourse in marriage as being recalcitrant refusal of a spiritual call. This tendency was condemned by the Church, sometimes from what might seem unlikely quarters. At the council of Nicaea in 325, the aged, ascetic monk Paphnutius, a disciple of Antony, staunchly defended the ideal of Christian marriage, affirming that a married man's intercourse with his wife deserved the name of chastity.

Even as God's salvation is realized personally, not generically, marriage, which points towards salvation, is a personal union. The spouses, who administer the sacrament of marriage to each other, are 'no longer two'; they become 'one flesh' (Mark 10.8). Theirs is an all-encompassing, ontological togetherness whose seal is definitive and therefore indissoluble. A graft is accomplished in marriage that cannot be woundlessly undone. 'A resolution is made,' wrote Ida Görres,

> that is realized in the slowness of a whole life. For the other, too, *is* not yet fully what he nonetheless *is*, but only embryonically. He must *become* it. For that purpose a lifetime is required, until our truest kernel has penetrated and conquered all the superficial and invalid layers of our self, until a human being truly

subsists, manifesting itself in truth. The fact that this inner self discerns the self in the other, and is bound and allied to the other, so that the two may help one another towards self-realization, this too is marriage.

A related insight is found in Marilynne Robinson's *Jack*, the fourth volume in what is (for now) her tetralogy extending from *Gilead*. When Della, the preacher's daughter, looks on Jack, she sees 'a soul, a glorious presence out of place in the world', almost disturbing in its brightness. Thanks to her seeing it, Jack becomes aware of it. He is, as it were, *seen* into being, drawn despite himself into conscious personhood. An inkling of this possibility had inhabited him since he first met Della. He knew there was something in her that uniquely called forth something in him.

In celebration of this fact, he performed one of his life's most uncharacteristic actions: one night, on his way back from work, he bought 'a small geranium plant with a red blossom on it and set it on his windowsill'. The geranium indicated that the bleak, featureless boarding-house room casually housing his dismal existence had, by virtue of another's loving sight, the makings of a garden.

While the early Church upheld and blessed the married state, it also fostered the state of consecrated virginity. The two may appear to stand in contradiction. But no. When I entered monastic life, an old monk said to me, 'Remember, you've no right to live a sterile life!' I have always been grateful for that remark. It qualifies celibacy and reveals its meaning. The celibate, no less than the married man or woman, is called to a generative life of communion, to see and to be seen, to love and to be loved; but where spouses are agents of communion to each other, the consecrated celibate surrenders unmediated to sacramental at-onement. He or she becomes a symbol of the Church, whose nuptial compact with Christ we have seen evoked in the Letter to the Ephesians.

The vocations to marriage and to the virginal state complement and illumine one another. This mutuality is spelled out in the prayer of consecration that crowns the perpetual, solemn profession of a Benedictine nun:

> This gift, Lord, has flowed into certain hearts from the fount of your liberality: no prohibition has diminished the honour of matrimony, and your first blessing remains upon its holy union, but you have granted that there should nonetheless be souls who, guided by your Providence, renounce the chaste bond of marriage. Desiring that mystery, they do not imitate the act of marriage but they love what it signifies.

'Chastity' is associated in like measure with the married and virginal state: there is no distinction of degree; both are blessed. Both require a degree of battle, like any elective affinity. To bind oneself to a privileged love is to order other loves, letting motions of the heart and flesh be tempered by a will illumined by grace and reason.

We may recall that 'virginity', in the language of the Church, is not exclusively a physiological definition. It also indicates a state of grace. States of grace are something we can grow into. In the offertory prayer considered above, humanity's recreation is hailed as being 'more wonderful still' than its creation. Something similar is said in a collect for the second week of Lent. It begins, '*Deus, innocentiae restitutor et amator*' ('God, restorer and lover of innocence'). 'Innocence' is more than pristine immaculateness. In the logic of grace it is something that can be restored. The same principle applies symbolically, *mutatis mutandis*, to virginity.

Virginity, to be fruitful, must be chosen as a vibrant option for *life*. It cannot be merely lugubrious resignation to sexual abstinence. We are culturally conditioned to think of virginity as pickled maidenhood. We associate it almost exclusively with women. The idea of masculine virginity provokes sniggers in our social context. A man who is a virgin is likely to dissimulate this fact, which carries social stigma. It is illuminating to consider an evocation of a man's resolve to embrace virginity. We find it in George Mackay Brown's many-layered novel *Magnus*. It tells the story of St Magnus of Orkney (1080–1117) with poetic licence, yet grounded in historical fact. It chronicles the crystallization of a man's supernatural call to live and die for Christ.

Mackay Brown struggled with this book. He referred to his manuscript as a 'gory battlefield'. He fought, and won. A key passage tells of a maturing that took place in the months preceding Magnus's journey across the sea to Trondheim to attend the burial of Erlend, earl of Orkney, whose corpse he would find laid out in the metropolitan cathedral, near St Olav's relics. That trip would seal Magnus's fate.

He is a young man, and handsome. His body, that spring, had taken 'a first kindling, blurrings of warmth and light'. He is ready for love, surrounded by the expectation that he will soon marry. A man of his standing lived to secure his own succession. Magnus desired this end, sanctified by God and affirmed by the very movement of nature that April: 'The hill was opened by the plough. Fire and earth had their way with one another. Was everywhere the loveliest spurting of seed and egg and spawn.' The Orkney landscape lay open as a parable of earthly felicity: 'The fires of creation. Out of the mingled fires of men and women come new creatures to people the earth. This is a good ordinance of God.'

In Magnus's heart, though, a competing ordinance speaks. He awakens to Christ's call. It bids him to abandon *everything* pertaining to this earth to obtain the pearl of great price, to be ready for that Marriage of which earthly marriage is an image. Magnus knows he must follow that call, though it causes pain, and not only to himself. A wife has been found for him, Ingerth. He does not, in the Biblical sense, 'know' her: 'The bed lay between them white and unbroken. Magnus slept in his own room. He dreamed. He was in a place of burnings and ice.' He hears a voice that addresses him, gentle and affirmative, but nonetheless exacting:

No, but there is love indeed, and God ordained it, and it is a good love and necessary for the world's weal, and worthy are those who taste of it. But there are souls which cannot eat at that feast, for they serve another and a greater love, which is to these flames and meltings (wherein you suffer) the hard immortal diamond. Magnus, I call thee yet once more to the marriage feast of the king.

'From that hour – it is said – Magnus enrolled himself in the company of virgins.'

The way he must walk to fulfil his call and become himself, avoiding 'missteps', involves the orientation of all his energy in one direction. A different fire is kindled in him, no less ardent than the first, yet other in kind: 'the fire that had long tormented the bridegroom began to harden to a cold precious flame. Fire and fire burned in their different intensities.'

Magnus's hallowed commitment does not make him unworldly. Celibacy is not meant to make men and women into angels. It is *one* way of making them gauge the depth of their humanity, which God assumed in order to make effective therein his love. Magnus explains this breaking-open of his being to his kind, warm-blooded friend Hold Ragnarson, mystified by Magnus's cold marriage:

> How shall I put it, my dear friend? It isn't that the rage of fire – which you so shrewdly observed in me in March and April – had died down. No, it is fiercer than ever. But it is no longer fixed on one object – the fertile conduit in the sweet flesh of woman – it has undergone a transmutation, it is diffused in a new feeling, a special regard for everyone who walks the earth, as if they all (even the tinkers on the road) were lords and princes. And this regard – it extends beyond human beings to the animals, it longs to embrace even water and stone. This summer I began to handle sea, shells, larks' eggs, a piece of cloth from the loom, with a delight I have never known before, not even as a child. You remember that morning last week when we fished with five Birsay men off Marwick Head. I had the helm myself. You remember that great lithe cod that was drawn in on the hook. Mans from Revay caught it. I was pierced with the beauty and the agony of the creature.

Having plumbed the depth of need, being touched *there* by the sanctifying, unifying power of God, Magnus comes to verify a personal bond with all creation that, for being spiritual, is manifest to him through the senses. He is alive to a new capacity for wonder and compassion. He is sensitive, too, to the secret agony of Ingerth, who, from being 'like a bee imprisoned in a burning window', wilts: 'Subtle witherings began to appear in her flesh before the summer was over.' It is one thing to adopt a fierce proposition for oneself, another to impose it on others. Magnus weeps at what he sees. Tears, he realizes, cannot be avoided in this world. Having asked, 'Is God to blame for all this suffering?', he corrects himself:

> What an empty question! Look at the agony on this crucifix I have round my neck. This crucifix is the forge, and the threshing-floor, and the shed of the net-makers, where God and man work out together a plan of utter necessity and of unimaginable beauty . . .

Hold 'smiled at the deep sincerity of his friend . . . at the beauty of the images he uttered . . . but in truth he was more perplexed than ever.'

What Magnus says makes sense, however. In love, we find ourselves by giving ourselves. The living water gushing up within us is made to be outpoured, not to be dammed up. For most, marriage is the school in which these lessons are learned. For some, they are acquired in consecrated solitude. For all, friendship is proof that nourishing intimacy can well be found in celibate relationships. Chaste giving and receiving is likewise at the heart of generative love. A pontifical statement on St Joseph, in whom the Church sees both a virgin and a spouse, reminds us:

> Being a father entails introducing children to life and reality. Not holding them back, being overprotective or

possessive, but rather making them capable of deciding for themselves, enjoying freedom and exploring new possibilities. Perhaps for this reason, Joseph is traditionally called a 'most chaste' father. That title is not simply a sign of affection, but the summation of an attitude that is the opposite of possessiveness. Chastity is freedom from possessiveness in every sphere of one's life. Only when love is chaste, is it truly love. A possessive love ultimately becomes dangerous: it imprisons, constricts and makes for misery. God himself loved humanity with a chaste love; he left us free even to go astray and set ourselves against him. The logic of love is always the logic of freedom.

Whether our generativity is biological or spiritual, we can take this counsel to heart.

A newly married couple crowned, oriented towards the altar on which is enacted the sacrifice by which Christ restored to humanity the robe of glory.

FREEDOM AND ASCESIS

Gunnel Vallquist, translator into Swedish of Marcel Proust, once inscribed for me her diary of the Second Vatican Council, which she covered from start to finish as a correspondent for the Swedish press. She wrote out Galatians 5.1: 'For freedom Christ has set us free.' That phrase represented for her, as it must for any Christian, the core of the Gospel and thereby of the Church's mission.

Does the Church's teaching on sex and chastity liberate? Many people think it does not. At this point, though, a couple of distinctions are called for.

First, we are muddled as to what it means to be 'free'. Ordinarily we think of freedom as scope to do what we feel like. We think in terms of freedom *from*, not of freedom *unto*. In Christian terms, freedom is about enabling commitment. The Biblical view of human nature, evidenced in Christ, regards the human being as essentially relational, oblative and covenantal. On this account, unhindered pursuit of momentary inclinations is not freedom. It is enslavement to whim, which, empirically speaking, rarely produces lasting happiness. Sensational thrills can come of it, true, but they are not much of a foundation on which to construct a life.

Secondly, the freedom Paul speaks of is of a specific sort: that for which Christ has set us free. This freedom presupposes a call to self-transcendence. The finality of life, Biblically speaking, is not limited to present thriving. Such thriving is a good, but by positing it as the be-all and end-all of existence, we sew ourselves up in our garments of skin. We lose sight of the robe of glory that alone reveals the sense of our yearnings and alone bears the promise of satisfying them.

Holiness, life everlasting, configuration to Christ, the resurrection of the body: these notions do not feature much, now, in people's thinking about relationships and sexuality. We have become alienated from the mindset that brought about the soaring verticality of the twelfth century's cathedrals, houses holding the whole of life while elevating it.

Was not a proposal recently made to fit a swimming pool on the rebuilt roof of Notre Dame de Paris? It seemed to me apt. It would symbolically have re-established the dome of water that sealed earth off from heaven on the first day of creation, before God's Image was manifest in it (cf. Genesis 1.7). It would have cancelled, again symbolically, the piercing of the firmament at Jesus's Baptism, which portended a new way of being human. Whatever fragment of mystery might remain within the church itself would have been performed beneath the splashing of bodies striving to perfect their form. The parable would have been significant.

Once the supernatural thrust has gone from Christianity, what remains? Well-meaning sentiment and a set of commandments found to be crushing, the finality of change they were meant to serve having been summarily dismissed.

Understandably, a movement will then be afoot to consign these to the archives. For what will be the point of them? Become this-worldly, the Church accommodates the world and makes herself reasonably comfortable within it. Her prescriptions and proscriptions alike will reflect and be shaped by current *mores*.

This calls for on-going flexibility, for secular society's *mores* change quickly, also in the sphere of liberal reflection on sex. Certain views propounded as liberating and prophetic well within living memory – regarding, for example, the sexuality of children – are now rightly seen as abhorrent. Yet new prophets are readily anointed, new theories put forward for experimentation in an area that touches us at our most intimate.

It is time to effect a *Sursum corda*, to correct an inward-looking, horizontalizing trend in order to recover the transcendental dimension of embodied intimacy, part and parcel of the universal call to holiness. Of course we should reach out to and engage those estranged by Christian teaching, those who feel ostracized or consider they are being held to an impossible standard. At the same time we cannot forget that this situation is far from new.

In the early centuries of our era, there was colossal strain between worldly and Christian moral values, not least concerning chastity. This was so not because Christians were better – most of us, now as then, live mediocre lives – but because they had a different sense of what life is about. Those were the centuries of the subtle christological controversies. Relentlessly, the Church fought to articulate who Jesus Christ *is*: 'God from God' yet 'born of the Virgin Mary'; fully human, fully divine. On this basis she went on to make sense of what it means to be a human being and to show how a humane social order might come about.

Today, Christology is in eclipse. We still affirm that 'God became man.' But we largely deploy an inverted hermeneutic, projecting an image of 'God' that issues from our garment-of-skin sense of what man is. The result is caricatural. The divine is reduced to our measure.

The fact that many contemporaries reject this counterfeit 'God' is in many ways an indication of their good sense.

What a contrast with earlier times. Nicholas Kavasilas, who lived at the time of Walter Hilton and Julian of Norwich, wrote:

> It was for the New Man that human nature was originally created; it was for him that intellect and desire were prepared. We received rationality that we might know Christ, desire that we might run towards him. For the old Adam is not a model for the new, but the new a model for the old.

In the midst of present perplexity, with the Church weighed down by a history of abuse, with society's deconstruction of categories that, just yesterday, we thought normative, and with no shortage of people who, like the peers of Isaiah, 'put darkness for light, sweet for bitter' (5.20), we need to be recalled to this perspective. The Desert Fathers' shortest dictum tells us to 'look up, not down.' The advice is sound. The Church, surely, is called to provide the compass by which people of good will might orient themselves in times of confusion, not to run after the crowds like a puffing old spaniel striving to keep up with the hunt.

This is not to say that the Church should condemn the world. 'Neither do I condemn you.' These words of Jesus addressed to the woman caught in adultery remain a norm to which any ambassador of Christ is held. So do the words that follow: 'Go your way, and from now on do not sin again' (John 8.11). Avoid wrong turns! The freedom for which Christ has set us free is freedom to follow him and to obtain the blessedness he has in store for us, not to get lost in the woods. The Church, said Pope John XXIII, is '*Mater et Magistra*'. As a teacher she has the duty to be clear; as a mother she is exacting, but tender and forbearing.

The Christian proposition of chastity is unattractive when put forward with rage or outrage, attitudes betraying self-righteousness on the part of its proponents. God, meanwhile, as John 8 shows, regards the affairs of human hearts and bodies with illusionless patience – though let us remember that 'patience' is more than a capacity to hang on and wait; at its heart is the root *patior*, which means 'I suffer.'

A compelling picture of God's patience is drawn in a short story by Marguerite Yourcenar. It features in her collection *Feux*, which instantiates nine paradigms of experience by evoking typical characters from literature. The paradigm of 'salvation' is represented by Mary Magdalene.

In Christian tradition, Mary Magdalene enters the scene of the Gospel drama as an incarnation of passion. Yourcenar, drawing on apocryphal sources, qualifies and complicates this outlook. In her story, Mary was betrothed to John. When John heeded Jesus's call, leaving her on the eve of their wedding, she felt betrayed. The One who claimed her lover as Beloved Disciple appeared to her a rival in the field of *eros*. She wanted revenge. She would take it by way of seduction, employing the dynamic of manipulative 'desire' that may colour, as we saw in our reading of Genesis 3-4, the relationship of woman and man in a fallen world.

When Christ was invited to dine in Simon the Pharisee's house, Mary struck. Potent in her charm, she entered the banqueting hall as a fury of passion, determined to claim for herself the Man she mockingly called 'God', who had stolen *her* man. Her purpose was to enact retaliation, playing on age-old allurements and fears.

> We sin because God is not. We opt for creatures because nothing that is perfect presents itself to us. As soon as John would understand that God was but a man, he'd have no reason to prefer him to my breasts. I adorned myself as for a ball; I doused myself with scent as for a bed. My entry into the banqueting hall caused people to stop chewing. The apostles stood up in a flurry. They feared that the rustle of my skirt would contaminate them. In the eyes of these good men, I was impure, as if continually bleeding. Only God stayed reclined on his leather couch. I instinctively recognized his feet, worn to the bone from walking the roads of our Sheol, his hair alive with the vermin of stars, his large, pure eyes like the one piece of heaven that remained with him. He was disfigured as grief, grimy as sin. I fell at his feet, swallowing my spittle. I could not add sarcasm to this terrible weight of God's sadness. I saw at once that I could not seduce him. For he did not flee from me. I untied my hair as if better to cover my fault's nakedness. Before him I poured out my phial of memories.

Christ does not flee from our contradictions. He does not shun in disgust the world of lusts and instant hopes that Siddhartha, in Hesse's novel, calls the world of 'people-who-are-like-children' (I once heard a seasoned confessor say, 'You know, there are no adults, only children'). He enters that world and calls out to us, 'Adam, where are you?' Sometimes he calls, as in Yourcenar's story, just by looking at us all-knowing, grieved at our estrangement, but not despairing of us.

We easily forget that God has hope for us. He knows we need to grow, and to grow up. In a reading of the Bible's protology that complements that of *The Cave of Treasures*, Irenaeus of Lyon presents Adam and Eve as children in the garden: 'man was a child, not yet having his understanding perfected; wherefore he was easily led astray.' But therefore, too, he had potential freely to grow, learn and change.

A Christian view of human nature is dynamic. Yes, of course we are conditioned by factors not subject to our choice; of course we carry gifts and wounds of all sorts; these condition us, but do not determine us. What determines a life is not the mould from which it issues but the goal towards which it moves. In Kavasilas's words, 'the old Adam is not a model for the new, but the new a model for the old.' If we believe this, we shall live prospectively, drawn by God's patient hope for us.

We are in the same boat. The second-century *Epistle to Diognetus* stresses that, left to ourselves, we are all borne along by 'disordered impulses [ἀτάκτοις φοραῖς], carried away by desires and cravings'. For some, disorder will be more patently 'objective' than for others. But all of us are called to re-orient our lives towards the finality revealed in Christ. In him fullness of life awaits us. Nowhere else.

After the death of Jean Daniélou in 1974, Gunnel Vallquist wrote an essay on 'The Daniélou Mystery'. She had known the cardinal very well. She set out, though, not from private recollection but from a subject of public prurience: how had it come about that he, a Prince of the Church, had died of a stroke in the flat of a Paris

prostitute, his wallet stacked with cash? Vallquist points
out that Daniélou had long ministered to women who
worked the streets of Batignolles. He helped them with
alms to care for their often complicated networks of
dependents. This work he carried on also after being
created a cardinal in 1969. For Daniélou, such contact,
illumined by Christian friendship, with people considered
to be beyond the pale was no big deal. So sharp, writes
Vallquist, was his awareness of the chasm that separates us
all from the uncreated glory of God that the calculation
of *degrees* seemed to him absurd. He did not, by being
a friend to prostitutes, relativize Catholic teaching: he
wrote strongly in defence of chastity. But he was not shy
to visit and assist those who, to reach this ideal, had a long
way to go. He was just acting like his Master.

The Christian condition is the art of striving to answer
a call to perfection while plumbing the depth of our
imperfection without despairing and without giving
up on the ideal. Cancelling the ideal is tantamount to
turning cathedrals into swimming pools, to replacing
Christ's personal call, 'Come, follow me' (Mark 1.17)
with a pre-printed message to 'take your ease, eat, drink,
and be merry' (Luke 12.19). The goal to which we are
called lies ever ahead. To stagnate is deadly.

But what if I have no strength to walk, never mind to
set out from the musty plains of Cain's *gyrovague* children
to scale the slope leading back to Mount Paradise? Well,
I must learn to let myself be carried. Israel's exodus, that
exemplarily tortuous voyage during which the people tried
every trespass, issued in the profession: 'Underneath are
the everlasting arms' (Deuteronomy 33.27). Providence,
Israel saw, had carried through thick and thin. Their
realization corresponded to the oracle God gave when

they stood on the Promised Land's threshold: 'the Lord your God bore you, as a man bears his son, in all the way that you went until you came to this place' (Deuteronomy 1.31), through all the waterless places.

The primary ascesis required of a Christian is trust. By trust we give up illusory claims to omniscience. We give ourselves into God's hands and choose to be reformed according to his purpose. Only he can realize his likeness in us, uniting in a chaste whole the disparate factors that make up our history and personality.

An error Christians have often made is to assume that chastity is somehow normal; but no, it is exceptional. Virtue does not come easily to us: when we try to practise it, we find that sin's wounds cut deep. They condition us to fail of our purpose. Even as we labour to learn charity, patience, courage and so forth, we must labour to become chaste, letting grace do its slow, transformative work. Short of fulgurant exceptions, growth in grace, like other growth, is organic. It happens slowly, secretly, we know not how (cf. Mark 4.27). But it does, in time, bear fruit.

Athanasius, in *On the Incarnation*, marvels at Christians who practise celibacy. For him, their witness is a sign of the end-times. Subsequently continence came to be taken for granted. Youths embracing the clerical or consecrated life were simply *expected* to be chaste, without always understanding what their physical passion, a gift from God, represents or how it might be channelled responsibly. Many have lived lives marked by division, as if the senses were pursuing an unruly life of their own to be either suppressed by force of will or anaesthetized.

Marguerite Yourcenar observes with regard to her Magdalene that the process by which vulnerability, desire and love are changed into supernatural attachment is not one of 'sublimation' but of orientation. I concur with her that 'sublimation' is 'in itself a very unfortunate term and one that insults the body'. What is at stake is something else: 'a dark perception that love for a particular person, so poignant, is often only a beautiful fleeting accident, less real in a way than the predispositions and choices that preceded it and that will outlive it'. How do we handle these?

Physical and affective impulses are ordered according to an attraction of soul made conscious through application of the mind. The integral reconciliation of our being ('integrity', we have seen, was long a synonym for 'chastity') presupposes an élan. In a psalm, the goal towards which Israel journeyed through the desert is described as 'the desirable land' (Psalm 105.24, Vulgate). The typology is timeless.

The single ascetic counsel St Benedict gives about chastity is 'Castitatem amare', 'Love chastity'. Only what I love will change me beautifully. Behaviours prompted by fear or disdain tend to disfigure. Love must be honed. The counsel on chastity is complemented by 'Ieiunium amare', 'Love fasting.' To refrain from feeding an appetite, even a physical hunger, can be a way of learning to love in an ordered, fruitful way.

I stress this aspect of learning. The Law, wrote St Paul to the Galatians, is a 'pedagogue' (3.24). The epistle's rhetoric makes us view the term critically. But to have a reliable pedagogue is splendid. In virtue, as in science and wisdom, we need to be taught. Our conscience must be formed. The point of Christian moral teaching is to outline a process of learning conceived of in terms of conversion and *ascesis*, i.e. 'exercise', a fitting metaphor in our society, which has a gym at every corner. The goal is freedom and thriving. To learn in this way is to see myself in terms of a reality that exceeds me. It is to be freed from imprisonment in my own limited notions.

Such work takes time. Patience is called for, and joy in every forward step. In terms of chastity, a quantum leap is made, for example, in progress from promiscuity to fidelity, whether or not the faithful relationship fully corresponds to the objective order of a nuptial union, sacramentally blessed, between man and woman. Every search for integrity is worthy of respect, deserving of encouragement.

The importance of intentionality in the way we deal with our affections and attractions is helpfully underscored by that quintessentially postmodern movement, LBGTQ+ – an ineffable acronym pointing towards a seemingly endless realm of possibility, like a secular appropriation of the *Tetragrammaton*. Its influence is felt in many ways, not least in pedagogy. In a 2022 manual used to teach Norwegian nine-year-olds about the facts of life, written by authors learned in cutting-edge research, children are taught that

> Gender identity is your own thought about who you are, and about how you see yourself. You can think of yourself as a boy or a girl without being entirely sure. You can wish to be called 'he', 'she', 'ze', or anything you like.

The vista is at first intoxicating: fancy being, and requiring others to accept one as, whatever one likes! The sense of excitement yields, though, to a weight of heaviness. Effectively a child is told to be a demiurge: to create reality anew according to his, her or zir self-perception there and then. Everything is possible, 'formless and empty', (cf. Genesis 1.2), waiting to be filled and ordered – by oneself at nine years of age.

Not long ago efforts were made to establish verifiable pathologies of sexual identity. Such categorization now seems terribly twentieth-century. The terms which the acronym LBGTQ+ suggests are self-subverting. For on this account, nothing is objective; choice is all, to be questioned by none. There is much room for confusion. A positive aspect is conceptual liberation from deterministic classifications. The creed, 'You can be whatever you like,' may awaken people to the scope of *becoming* that lies at the heart of Christian hope. The rainbow logo unwittingly reproduces a Biblical symbol whose message is: 'God is faithful' (cf. Genesis 9.13).

There is an eschatological thrust in the desire to overcome binary oppositions. Christ came to make the two one (cf. Ephesians 2.14, Galatians 3.28). Trouble ensues when human beings try to accomplish overcoming unaided. Christianity entertains hope of transcending human dichotomies not through pendular alterations, but through a transfiguration in love that realizes our thirst for infinity through graced communion with Infinite Being. A Christian should naturally honour what is good in the aspirations of secular anthropology. He or she should also correct its presumption. Christians know a lot about presumption. From the beginning, presumption has caused humankind to veer off course. It has a way of detaching us from what is real. Still, the havoc wrought by man's attempts to be self-made may yet lead us back to a taste for lasting, carrying truth.

Grounded in truth, we can reach immense stature. The life that pulsates in us carries an echo of God even when bogged down in self-destructive patterns. St John Climacus, abbot of Mount Sinai during the pontificate of Gregory the Great, speaks of the maturing he has observed in people caught up in what nowadays we would call sexual addiction:

> I have watched impure souls mad for physical love but turning what they know of such love into a reason for penance and transferring that same capacity for love to the Lord. I have watched them master fear so as to drive themselves unsparingly towards the love of God. That is why, when talking of that chaste harlot, the Lord does not say, 'because she feared', but rather, 'because she loved much', she was able to drive out love with love (ἔρωτι ἔρωτα διακρούσασθαι).

It is an astonishing statement. It effectively dismantles the view that would separate spiritual *eros* from carnal *eros*. For Climacus, they belong to a single continuum. He calls on 'the chaste harlot' to witness his thesis. Yourcenar would approve. This perspective does not 'insult the body'. It offers neither sublimation nor appeasement. It acknowledges a flicker of eternity in passion. Even disordered *eros* can kindle a sanctifying love of God that drives out fear. Nothing is beyond God's ordering power. Nothing in man is unredeemed. Everything natural to man is made in view of the robe of glory. The new Adam waits to embrace the old. The garments of skin are lent us for a while, to warm and protect us. Then we are to leave them behind.

People in the Middle Ages were sensitive to the many-layered significance of Mary Magdalene. What gracefulness in this French statue from the fifteenth century! Mary Magdalene would be an excellent patron saint for the twenty-first.

* * *

So these are some tensions through which the way to chastity passes. It is good to think about them, but they cannot be resolved in our heads. A dialectical model of thesis and antithesis striving for synthesis is of limited use. We must live these tensions, grow through them. New dimensions of experience will open up before us. Chastity, which initially can seem to spell constraint, will reveal itself as broad strength full of sweetness. The priest reminds himself of this each day when he vests for Mass. Putting on his girdle he prays for the gift of purity, '*ut maneat in me virtus castitatis*', 'that the strength of chastity may abide in me'. To get even a foretaste of this strength, to see it alive in others, is to wish to possess it fully. It frees the body, broadens the heart, illumines the mind, balancing the three.

With this finality in mind, the tensions specific to each one of us may seem less forbidding. They may even reveal an attraction once we realize the purpose they serve, once we are governed by the Word who brings *kosmos* out of chaos. There is light to be found in the friendly words Rilke wrote to Kappus on 16 July 1903, printed in the volume of letters Etty Hillesum kept under her pillow in Westerbork:

I would like to beg you, dear Sir, as well as I can, to have patience with everything that is unsolved in your heart and to try to cherish the questions themselves, like closed rooms and like books written in a very strange tongue. Do not search now for the answers which cannot be given you because you could not live them. It is a matter of living everything. Live the questions now. Perhaps you will then gradually, without noticing it, one distant day live right into the answer.

Negotiating Passion

In 1982 the Indian-Catalan priest Raimundo Panikkar published *Blessed Simplicity: The Monk as Universal Archetype*. The fact that this book was so widely read and translated suggests the author's thesis is well-founded. Many women and men recognize in themselves some aspects of the call which the monk or nun instantiates. Monastic experience carries universal relevance, for it is rooted in deep humanity.

Western literature is rich in archetypal monastic characters. We might think of Dostoyevsky's Zosima, Hesse's Narcissus, Bernanos's Blanche de la Force or Diderot's *Religieuse*. Even in northern Europe, where monasticism was wiped out in the violent sixteenth century, the figure of the monk kept a certain fascination. We find a monk's haunting presence in Knut Hamsun's novel *Victoria*. This monk, Vendt, occurs in a poem internal to the book, so is explicitly fictional, yet he matters to the plot. His creator, the writer of the poem, is a poor miller's son aspiring to literary greatness. He sits in a town garret working on a masterpiece about love. Vendt, the monk, illustrates for him passion's animal, instinctive power. 'Ah', sighs Vendt,

does not love transform the human heart into a mushroom patch, a voluptuous and shameless garden in which there grow secretive, impertinent mushrooms!

Does it not cause the monk to roam through gardens
enclosed and peek through the windows of sleepers at
night? Does it not possess the nun with madness?

Hamsun's monastics are far removed from Panikkar's
inclusive spirituality. The monk represents frustrated
sexuality, a feverish voyeurism exercised under the cover
of night's darkness. As for the nun, she is a love-deprived
lunatic.

This caricature is still in vogue. The abuse crisis has
consolidated it. It may, then, come as a surprise to learn
that monasticism's sources, its textbooks, are concerned
with the wise negotiation of passion. This literature is
based on the conviction that every desire, even the most
embodied, is a glimmer of a longing for God imprinted on
our being, created in God's image. A monastic approach
to passion does not seek to block it, but to channel it,
so to generate the verve required on our journey towards
God while we patiently drain the mushroom-infested,
boggy patches of our lives, which have become unfruitful
on account of passionate overspill.

I wish to look at a few key themes on the basis of the
sayings of the Desert Fathers, collections of apodictic
wisdom from the fourth and fifth centuries, born of
conversations among monks as they sought useful answers
to timeless questions.

The ascetic life was in this period a novelty. The first
monks retired to the desert without much of a structure
to lean on. They saw themselves as followers of Abraham,
who at the Lord's behest set out from Mesopotamia to go
he knew not where; or like the Israelites leaving Egypt,
led by an angel of God through the wilderness. What they
did have was the Bible. They knew it well. Their purpose

and hope was to let the Biblical drama of redemption be realized in their own lives.

The Apophthegmata are a user's manual for Scripture. How can I let God's Word strike root in me? How can I apply it to my experience? How is Christ's saving work realized in particular lives? These questions exercised the brothers who came to see an *abba*, a seasoned elder, asking for a 'word' to live by. Thus, as I have said, the monastic institute turned into something of a laboratory for Christian doctrine and practice.

Athanasius's *Life of Antony*, for instance, can be read as evidence to prove that the dogma set out in the patriarch's treatise *On the Incarnation* actually works. Athanasius shows how the life of a person like you and me is changed by Christ's mystery as the Church expounds it. He presents the new monastic Israel as a company of heralds ushering in a new aeon. The monks drag humanity a bit further up the mountain from which it once descended in thrall to appetite and ignorance, resensitizing it to a nostalgia for Eden.

To illustrate the change humanity has undergone in Christ, Athanasius adduces the evidence of celibate chastity. 'For who among men', he asks,

> whether after death or even while alive has offered a teaching about virginity and has not considered such a virtue impossible to practise for human beings? However, our Saviour and King of all, Christ, taught so powerfully on this subject that even youngsters who have not yet come of age profess a virginity that transcends the law.

It is axiomatic to him that such profession is the work of God: only continued consent to grace enacted by means of enlightened choices embedded in a coherent life can keep this commitment alive as a source of beatitude and fruitfulness.

St Antony certainly did not look like Zurbaran imagined him in this painting, now in the Hulton Fine Art Collection, produced around 1640. It is pleasing all the same, with the Father of Monks got up more or less like a Cistercian. 'Let Christ be the air you breathe,' said Antony to his brothers on his deathbed.

The Call to Perfection

What caused men and women in the early Christian centuries to relinquish property, status and family to devote themselves full-time to the search for God in the monastic state? These days we would posit a *vocation* requiring discernment; indeed, a mystique of discernment has emerged, as if being in discernment were a vocation in its own right. We largely look in vain for such a quest in early Christian literature. The Desert Fathers tend to be matter-of-fact, practical, even pragmatic in accounts of their life choice. They rarely invoke Damascus Road epiphanies. What they do speak of is a rational decision to follow Christ without compromise.

For some, hearing a word of Scripture proved decisive. Antony the Great set out on his journey after hearing Jesus's words to the rich young man: 'If you would be perfect, sell what you own, and follow me' (Matthew 19.21). The words pierced him; he was certain they were *for him*. For others, remembrance of baptism was a motivating factor. Abba Gregory spells out what this sacrament requires of any baptized Christian: 'As far as the soul is concerned, right faith; as far as the tongue is concerned, truth; as far as the body is concerned, temperance' (I.3). He saw that life in the world made it hard to live up to this standard. So he went into the desert.

Once our eyes have been opened to faith as something real, a reorientation of existence is called for. Faith in the Son of God made man requires of me an embodied response, made concrete in a life of conversion, not just in the rehearsal of abstract sublimities. 'Be perfect,' said the Lord (cf. Matthew 5.48). This summons is intrinsic to a Christian perception of discipleship. A brother once asked Abba Macarius what perfection was about. The *abba* answered:

Unless a man obtains great humility of both heart and body, so that he entirely ceases to compare himself with others and rather submits humbly to every creature, without judging anyone other than himself; unless he endures insult and weeds out every trace of evil from his heart, while forcing himself to be patient and of benefit to others, a friend to his brethren, temperate and master of himself; unless he uses his eyes to see what is right; unless he guards his tongue and averts his ear from all useless speech that harms the soul; unless he works righteousness with his hands, keeping his heart pure and his body immaculate before God; unless he keeps death before his eyes daily and renounces all anger, all spiritual evil; unless he renounces the lust of matter and the flesh, as well as the devil and all his works; unless he binds himself steadfastly to God, the King of the universe, and to all his commandments, so to remain close to God at all times, in all circumstances, in all his occupations; well, then he has no chance of approaching perfection (I.16).

These are not banal requirements. They were understood, as they must be, to be obligatory and non-negotiable. When men and women left familiar lives and set out for the desert, it was to avoid the most obvious temptations and distractions, so that they might focus all energy on striving towards the one thing necessary.

In this regard, I should underline a couple of points. First: even if monasticism was seen as a help to Christian perfection, it was never regarded as holding a monopoly on perfection. The literature refers again and again to austere monks sent by God's Spirit to meet, say, a cobbler in Alexandria or a clown in Antioch, folk who, in the middle of the city's bustle, had attained greater perfection than they. Secondly: the monk is not permitted, even for a second, to nurture illusions that he makes progress towards an evangelical life under his own steam. Abba Marcos sums up the insight of tradition when he says that it is not human virtue, but alone Christ's cross, that enables Christians to serve perfectly under the law of perfect freedom (I.17).

The motivation underlying a decision to embrace the pursuit of perfection is, then, objective and rational. It springs from a desire to follow the Gospels and to live up to obligations contracted at baptism. At the source is a decision rooted in free will, carried by faith. This is later instilled with spiritual desire, so that affectivity can make its contribution. An experienced monk wrote lyrically of the blessed repose – *hesychia* – which establishes the tonality of the monk's desire for God:

> O repose! Every day, every night you await Christ while keeping the lamp from going out. You desire him and sing incessantly: 'My heart is ready, O God, my heart is ready!' . . . O repose, Christ's field: wonderful is the harvest you bear!' (II.35).

This repose is a function of the soul's reconquered harmony. It expresses our true human nature, which only through sin's alienation becomes chaotic and violent.

To refer to sin, the Fathers sometimes (e.g. V.46) use the word πλημμέλημα [*plēmmelēma*]. It literally means 'a striking of wrong notes'. Our authentic being is sweet music to the Lord. Only when we are no longer faithful to ourselves, does dissonance arise.

What is required of us is not to transcend human nature, as if we had to leave our incarnate self behind to become angelic. No! The transformation the Fathers had in mind was a reconquest of true humanity. One who would serve God, said Abba Poimen, 'must refrain from all that militates against his nature, that is to say, against anger, irritation, hatred and slander of his brother; from all that pertains to the past' (I.21). What should interest us is what lies ahead. In Ephesians, St Paul speaks of the Christian's call 'to mature manhood, to the measure of the stature of the fulness of Christ' (4.13). The Apophthegmata have this finality in mind when they say: ὅρος χριστιανοῦ μίμησις Χριστοῦ, a dense phrase I can only render paraphrastically: 'The measure of the Christian is his – or her – imitation of Christ' (I.37). We approach perfection in so far as Christ lives in us so that his life becomes ours.

REST IN UNREST

The repose I have spoken of is no sweet slumber. On the contrary, it presupposes battle. Abba Antony states this squarely: 'He who lives in the desert in repose [ἡσυχάζων] is freed from three kinds of battle: the battles of hearing, speech, and sight. He is concerned with only one, namely the battle of the heart' (II.2). The monk escapes worldly distraction in order to attend to voices that arise from within in the form of intimate thoughts, temptations and desires.

A Desert Father once demonstrated the foundation of contemplative life by means of a physics experiment. When asked what the benefit was of living far from the haunts of men, he poured water into a bowl and told the enquirers: 'Look at the water!' They looked, but saw nothing: the water was muddy. After a while, the *abba* said: 'Look again at the water.' His visitors did as they were told and, true enough, 'they saw their own faces as in a mirror.' The *abba* then said, 'This is the way of one who lives in the middle of others; on account of all the unrest, he is unable to see his own sin. But once he finds repose [ὅταν δὲ ἡσυχάσῃ], above all here in the desert, his eyes are opened to all his failings' (II.29). Ascetic rest reveals the heart's unrest. The budding contemplative must learn to deal with this first.

What is the source of unrest? Memories, above all. An experienced nun once told me she had spent her first years in the monastery with the sense that all she had hitherto lived through was projected on an interior cinema screen. She had to sit through the entire performance, without a fast-forward option. This experience is typical for novices. As soon as we unplug outward providers of visual and auditive impressions, a corresponding bombardment of impressions begins from within. We had no idea we were carrying them all. Experiences, images, words and emotions we thought (and possibly wished) we had forgotten are drawn forth in a flood of remembrance. The scene is potentially set for an experience of Aristotelian *catharsis*, but a version of *me* is the protagonist of the drama I am watching.

St Mary of Egypt, who spent an energetic career as a prostitute in Alexandria for seventeen years, told Abba Zossima that she lived, after her conversion, with vivid mental and physical memories of her professional life for a corresponding seventeen years. This sort of baggage, tradition tells us, must be dispatched; it is well to get the job done before we find ourselves at check-in. For that to happen, we must sit still and look at ourselves as we are. When Abba Moses told a monk to remain in his cell faithfully, 'and the cell will teach you everything' (II.19), this is the sort of thing he had in mind. To learn to know God, we must first know ourselves. That is not always easy. Abba Dioscoros said: 'If I could truly see my sins, the

strength of five men would not suffice to bewail them.'
Abba Poimen, who tells the story, adds: 'This is what a
man is like who knows himself' (III.23).

Patience is required to live in this way; courage, too.
Still, the stilled water in the desert monk's bowl offers
encouragement. Abba Nilos reassures us:

> Any passion which is not actively stimulated will
> gradually move towards greater temperance, and will
> eventually cease entirely. With time it loses strength.
> When the passionate inclination is gone, only
> remembrance of the deed remains (II.23).

Here we find two insights of capital importance for
anyone aspiring to chastity. First, Abba Nilos ascertains
that any passionate thought or deed leaves a mark – and
remember, the 'passions' the Fathers spoke of were not
just sexual, but likewise referred to wrath, envy and so
forth. An actively nurtured passion lives in us like a
vital principle, an autonomous impulse. 'A habit', the
Apophthegmata insist, 'which is strengthened over time
acquires the force of nature': the ἔθος [ethos] masquerades
as φύσις [physis] (IV.67), so that it can be hard to tell
one from the other. It is obvious that we must be on
our guard with regard to the impressions we admit into
our heart and mind. To get rid of them once they are
there is easier said than done. The second insight is this:
destructive passions *can* be starved to death, provided
we take responsibility for them and deliberately reject
them, all with God's help, naturally. The remembrance
of sin remains. But once the sting has been excised, it
is harmless. It can even be of benefit, spurring us on
towards humility.

To See Clearly

We have looked at the shock of grace that may cause a man or woman to wish to begin a new life. We have considered ways of dealing with wounds from the past. What of the way forward here and now? It is marked by an ongoing battle against primary impulses that, in the sense in which, above, we defined 'sin', would draw the monk away from his true goal.

These impulses may seem primitive, but are in reality most subtle. Also, they are interconnected. For this reason the Fathers may, for instance, recommend a period of fasting to fight irritability; or exercises in humility to overcome erotic temptation. Instead of considering the passions in isolation, they developed an overall strategy to underpin ascesis.

This strategy is rooted in an endeavour concerned with seeing. The monk strives, first, to see his desire for what it is in order to see himself in truth. Secondly, he would see his fellow men and women with Christian clarity. Thirdly, he hopes to see God on the terms set out by the Beloved Disciple, not on the basis of human projections, but 'as he is' (1 John 3.2). Let us consider these three aspirations in turn.

How do I see myself as I am? First, I must identify and name the factors that motivate the options that shape my life. Next, I must own the consequences of these options. We find a matter-of-fact example of what this might mean in a story attributed to Abba Zeno. Zeno recounts how, one torridly hot day, he found himself walking past a cucumber field. He was hungry and thirsty. We know from the Pentateuch how appetizing cucumbers can be for desert wanderers (cf. Numbers 11.5). Zeno stood by the fence and looked at the crop, his mouth dried out.

There was no doubt about what he *wanted*. He did not, however, simply give in to his appetite. Instead he asked himself lucidly: 'Am I then strong enough to sustain the punishment a thief deserves?' The cucumbers, after all, were someone else's. In order to find out, he took up position right there, under the scorching sun, as if placed in the stocks. After five days he could not stand it any more. 'Therefore he said to his thought: "If you cannot [bear the sanction you deserve], don't steal, and don't eat."'

Note: 'he said *to his thought*.' The thought in question was the voice of concupiscence saying, 'Go on: have a cucumber! The sun is harsh, you are worn out, and the farmer has lots.' Zeno refused to identify himself with that thought. He related to it the way we would relate to a telephone sales agent: he would not hear of an investment (in the form of action) until he knew exactly what the proposal might entail. To find out, he gave up five days of his life.

Did he not have better things to do: baskets to weave, prayers to say? No doubt he did. But nothing seemed to him more important than to reach clarity regarding the voice in his heart (IV.17). We have seen how a habit that is strengthened over time can acquire the force of nature. In Zeno's case we see a staunch refusal to allow an *ethos* (even one as innocent as thirst on a hot day) to overwhelm his *physis*. To tell one from the other, he applied reason.

The Fathers would call this approach sane, responsible and *human*. Variations on the theme can be found in different keys throughout the literature. Another monk felt tempted to leave the desert to find himself a wife. 'Oh well', he said to himself: 'so you want to get married? But have you strength to ensure the upkeep of a wife and children?' Without further ado, he made two figures of clay and said: 'Here is your wife. Here is your son. From now on you must work twice as hard, that they may live.' After a few days he was exhausted. He concluded: 'If you haven't the strength to maintain a family, you shouldn't acquire one' (V.50).

We may smile as such stories. They seem to us naïve, and so they are; not in the sense the adjective has acquired in current speech (connoting gullible), but in its original sense of 'uncontaminatedly lucid' – *naïf* is derived from *nativus*. The Fathers refused to rationalize their desires. They considered them concrete proposals with concrete impact. This was true not least for passion in its most embodied form. The Apophthegmata deal fearlessly with *porneia*, the wide spectrum of sexual temptation. They display a reflexivity that may amaze us, accustomed as we are to explicit but often superficially pondered engagement with such issues.

Here, too, it matters to *see* what – and whom – one is dealing with; indeed, it is paramount to see, not just to listen. Once a young brother came to an *abba* in despair at his unclean thoughts. Why, he cried, was he not helped by grace when he was praying all the time? The elder, enlightened by God's Spirit, saw what was going on: the young man had indeed tried to pray, but had nonetheless remained sitting next to the demon of impurity, chatting with it in between devotions. Nearby stood God's angel powerless, since the brother would not be helped. Graced with this insight, the old monk was able to teach the young man how to act. His advice was simple: 'Don't engage in talk!' (V.23). In the heat of battle he should not try to understand or persuade his opponent, nor try to make sense of tempting thoughts. Rather he should be alert to their provenance. 'As soon as they begin to speak, you must withhold your answer; instead rise, throw yourself on the ground and say, "Son of God, have mercy on me!"' (V.37). The early monks knew that the demon of impurity rarely shows its face. It talks sweetly. It seems reasonable. Yet tradition insists: if by grace we get to see it face to face, we find that 'it stinks' (V.27).

The Desert Fathers were not, on the whole, dualists hostile to the body. Abba Antony speaks for mainstream tradition when he says that the body's impulses as such are natural and morally neutral. Yet a twisted, passionate urge can cause these impulses to diverge from nature. This urge appears in two forms. The first is purely physical. It comes about when we pamper our bodies voluptuously. This is why the pursuit of chastity is inseparable from fasting, which we should understand not merely as disciplined eating but as a psychobiological, therapeutic practice of liberation from self-centredness. The second form of the passionate urge is spiritual, born of the devil's jealousy (V.1). The father of lies does not want us to be sanctified in truth. He confounds us where we are most vulnerable.

A sign of a given temptation's diabolical origin is its tendency to induce hopelessness. A monk who falls prey to it thinks that he is abandoned by God; that for him there can be no pardon. This is the *greatest* temptation. The Apophthegmata praise monks who, in battle against impurity, refuse to abandon hope of God's grace (V.47). Even the darkest thoughts are powerless if we do not grant them entry to our heart. We are safe as long as we refuse to be impressed. Trouble begins the moment we close our eyes and entrust ourselves to the tempter's soft voice, which draws us into the realm of chaos from which it issues.

What about seeing my brother – the representative and present *other* – in truth? To introduce this topic, we may consider a story about Macarius the Great:

It was said about Abba Macarius the Great that he, on a journey through the desert, found a skull lying on the ground. The elder touched it with his staff and said: 'And you, who are you? Answer me!'

The skull answered: 'I was high priest of the pagans here in this place. And you are Abba Macarius, bearer of the Spirit. When you have pity on those who are punished [beyond the grave], they are comforted a little.'

Abba Macarius asked: 'Wherein does this comfort consist?'

The skull answered: 'As far as heaven is from earth, so far fire extends under our feet and under our head; when we stand in the middle of the fire, we cannot see each other face to face, for we are bound back to back. But when you pray for us, each of us can glimpse the face of the other.'

The elder wept and said: 'Woe to the day on which man was born, if this is what counts as comfort in eternal torment!' (III.19).

We need not be detained by the technical challenges the text throws up (why and how are the damned tied back to back?); we are dealing with a fraught manuscript tradition with many variants. What matters is this: damnation is conceived of as inability to see the face of others. It spells the annihilation of personhood, a state in which a person's identity is reduced to, and enclosed in, mere individuality.

A damned human being, cut off from God, is consumed by loneliness. A holy human being, in contrast, one living in communion with the triune God, is utterly *personal*. Oriented towards the other in purity and love, he or she carries blessing right into hell.

The Fathers drew practical consequences from this sublime theology, applying it to daily life. We constantly read of situations in which the question is whether one person *sees* his fellows or really has eyes only for himself. The examples are of perennial relevance. Epiphanios, a monk who had become bishop of Cyprus, once invited his old friend Abba Hilarion to visit when they were both of a great age. While they were talking, the bishop's housekeeper served a nice roasted bird. Hilarion declined politely but firmly, saying, 'Forgive me, Abba, but since receiving the habit, I have not eaten meat.' The bishop responded, 'And I, since I was clothed, have never let another go to rest [at night] with something against me, even as I have never gone to rest with something against another.' 'Forgive me, Abba', said Hilarion, 'your way of life is higher than mine' (IV.15).

What is more important here: my high principles or delicate attention with regard to a friend? The story implies that the superior ascesis consists in courtesy, a high form of self-transcendence.

We find this principle more drastically illustrated in the story of a young monk tormented by impure thoughts. When he went to an *abba* to open his heart, the old man, in spite of his grey hair and beard, turned out to be ἄπειρος [*apeiros*], 'without experience': he violently scolded the brother and told him that a man who entertains such thoughts is unworthy of the monk's habit. The young disciple was saddened, lost heart and decided to abandon monastic life. Thank God, on his way back into the world, he ran into Abba Apollos. Apollos was a perceptive man. He had eyes to see. He noticed at once the brother's burden of sadness, and asked, 'But child, why are you so downcast?' The young monk told his story. Apollos consoled him:

'Child, this is nothing to be astonished about. Don't give up hope! I myself, ancient as I am, am often plagued terribly by thoughts! Don't lose courage on account of a fever which no human zeal, but only God's mercy can heal. Give me a day or so, then you can return to your cell.'

The young man settled down, heartened, while Apollos took his staff and went to pay a visit to his old colleague, the one who had been harsh. Taking position outside this man's cell, Apollos prayed: 'Lord, you let temptations come to those who may benefit from them. Let [my young] brother's battle be transferred onto this old man so that he . . . may experience what a long life has not taught him, so to show mercy to those who do combat.' Apollos's prayer was heard. Forthwith the old man came running out of his door, shouting 'like a drunkard', unable to endure the temptation, running for the world. Apollos stopped him and explained what was going on. With high sarcasm he said, 'Probably the devil thought you unworthy of temptation, and that is why you were cruel to the brother who was having a hard time' (V.4).

This story teaches us a lot: that the weakness of the flesh is a universal experience; that sexual temptations are composite; that temptation can serve a useful purpose if it leads us into humility; that acquaintance with our own weakness teaches us compassion with others; and that we, when we see another human being in truth – weak but with capacity for and will towards the good – see him or her the way God sees them, that is, with infinite mercy.

As for the quest to see God, the passage of sixteen centuries has removed nothing of the pathos of Abba Isaiah's lament: 'Woe is me! For your name surrounds me, yet I serve your enemies!' (III.13). To be surrounded by God's name is to live in God's presence. To live in God's presence, though, is not tantamount to seeing God; and if we do not see God we are prone to forget that he is there, surrounding us.

The Beatitudes proclaim that God is visible to the pure of heart. Monastic wisdom takes this reference seriously. Cassian saw purity of heart as the goal of monastic life. If we set out to reach it, a long way opens up before us. It has rough patches. Often, contemplation of God is perceptible first as an experience of absence. What I long for seems so remote. Increasingly, I come to see that the absent one is not God, but I. I am the one who has left the Father's house and gone off into a far country. Having come to my senses, I can start the work of conversion and repentance.

It is not primarily the memory of particular sins that forms the basis for repentance, the joy-bearing *penthos* to which the Fathers aspired. This sorrow, made explicit in the beatitude of weeping, is wholly unlike depressive *tristesse*. The monk sorrows blessedly in so far as he discovers whom he has wounded by his faithlessness; in so far as he realizes God's immense philanthropy. Abba Isaac once saw Abba Poimen in ecstasy at prayer. 'Where, Abba, was your thought?' he asked afterwards. Poimen said, 'Where St Mary stood and wept at the Saviour's cross. How I desire to weep like that always!' (III.31).

Of the fulfilment of contemplative longing the Apophthegmata speak with restraint. '*Secretum meum mihi*' is what the desert's sons and daughters murmur still in response when we, intrusive gawkers, become too curious: 'My secret is my own' (cf. Isaiah 24.16 in the Vulgate). Even the holiest monks insist that they have hardly begun to work on their conversion. Still, we get a faint idea of what it means to see God when, now and again, we catch a glimpse of transformed lives.

The monastic life is lived in the light of Christ's resurrection. 'About Abba Arsenios it was said that he, on Saturday evening, while the glory of Sunday readied itself, turned his back to the sun and, hands raised towards heaven, remained standing thus, praying, until the sun illumined his face' (XII.1). This sabbath vigil from sunset to sunrise displays the monk's vocation and purpose. His attention is drawn towards the east from which Christ, according to his promise, will return. When existence is oriented, eternity's light reveals its splendour in transitory vessels.

When Abba Lot asked Abba Joseph about the sense of Christian asceticism, 'the elder arose, extended his hands towards heaven, and his fingers became like ten glowing lamps. Then he said, "If you wish, you can become fire entirely"' (XII.9). The God whom the desert ascetics longed to see has become man in Christ; faith in the incarnation saturates their lives. Further, when the monks, with the words of the Psalms, cried out, 'Lord, show me your face!', they were conscious that the Lord has a way of manifesting himself in human faces. At the end of his long life, Abba Antony said: 'I no longer fear God. I love him' (XVII.1). He had become living proof that love *can* drive out fear. He had become an icon of Christ, irresistibly beautiful. When the aged Antony asked a visiting disciple what he could do for him, the young man said, 'Father, it is enough for me to see you' (XVII.5). In Antony's features he discerned evidence of God's present agency. He saw what he himself was called to become.

The texts we have considered put forward an ideal relevant for all of us. They reveal how eyes are opened, how the Lord may answer *us* when we pray with blind Bartimaeus, 'Lord, that I might see!' (Mark 10.51). The beginning of living chastely in the world is to see it as it is, with reverence, desiring to encounter what I see, but freed from the need to possess.

Such seeing is grace. Grace presupposes endeavour. I must shed habits that obscure and weigh down my nature, created light in order to be light. To see truly is to be changed by what I see. It is important to remember this in a climate inducing me to think that reality ought to adapt itself to me, not I to it.

The classical terminology of passions and ascesis, *ethos* and *physis*, sprang from a yearning to recapture what is natural to man, created in God's image, called to realize his likeness. Formed by Christ's commandments, the desert ascetics declared war on all in them that compromised their dignity and beauty as sons and daughters of God. They took it for granted that the divine image imprinted on their being was marred. But they were certain that God could restore it to full splendour. The aim of monastic life, according to Panayotis Nellas, is 'to retrace the path of Adam in reverse, to cleanse the "garments of skin", and to raise the functions of their existence to the level of the natural iconic functions which existed before the fall'. All Christians are called to follow this path, according to their state of life. The one true, worthy goal of human life is the *redeemed* love of God and neighbour that transforms our being and makes it Godlike.

In calculating, risk-averse times it is hard to see life as a process of conversion, healing and change. It is counter-cultural to live with empty hands and to tread this earth chastely, freed from the will to domineer. We may think this bright ideal so far out of reach that we stop striving for it and languish in cocooned darkness. We need the testimony of the Fathers. It reminds us: 'If you wish, you can become fire.'

Contemplative Life

From my eyes must fall scales that turn my gaze merely inward towards *my* needs, *my* desires. There is resonance in Christ's saying, 'If anyone looks upon a woman in order to lust, he has already committed adultery with her in his heart' (Matthew 5.28). The key element here is the preposition πρός [*pros*], 'in order to'. What is evoked is not a spontaneous encounter with beauty stirring a response at once of mind and body. Such experience is not necessarily unchaste. It simply reveals man as man, woman as woman. It can issue in wonder and thanksgiving, be full of joy, lead to love. The subject of the Gospel's sanction is one who has aroused in himself a hunger for satisfaction, then looks for an object to feed on. In so far as there is sexuality in this scene, it is present as self-centred appetite. The beholder scans his surroundings not as a seeker after fellowship, but as a consumer; his focus is on his lust, not on the other. And this, says Christ, is unworthy of a human being. It debases the prowling subject and humiliates the sought object, present only as flesh.

As the antidote to such predatory looking, the Gospel presents the example of luminous seeing: 'The eye is the lamp of the body. So, if your eye is sound, your whole body will be full of light' (Matthew 6.22). The adjective

Matthew uses to describe an eye working as it should is ἁπλοῦς [*haplous*]. It forms a pair with διπλοῦς [*diplous*]. This pair corresponds to the Latin word-pair *simplex-duplex*. What makes the eye sound is the fact of being simple, that is, integral. A good case could be made for translating, 'So, if your eye is chaste, your whole body will be full of light.'

This way of seeing is proper to infants. It always moves me viscerally when such a little one looks me straight in the eye, unblinking and unafraid, curiously benevolent and expecting benevolence, open to take in and freely absorb the surrounding world. I once looked out on reality like that; we all did. Do you remember? I would love to see it that way once more.

Happily, chaste seeing can be re-learned. Or rather, a simple, unmingled eye can be re-acquired. St Bruno assured his friend Raoul of this during his life's last decade. Settled in Calabria, he explained the nature of the Carthusian call:

> What benefit and divine gladness the desert's solitude and silence reserve for those who love it, only those who have experienced it can know. Here, the strong can enter into themselves and remain there, with themselves, as much as they like, diligently cultivating seeds of virtue and eating happily the fruits of paradise. Here, they can acquire the eye whose serene gaze wounds the Bridegroom with love. Such an eye, being pure and uncontaminated, allows them to see God.

Raoul will have picked up Bruno's allusion to Gregory the Great's life of St Benedict. The beginnings of Benedict's retreat from the world are described there with the words,

'*Solus habitavit secum,*' 'He lived alone with himself.' We have encountered this motif before: to see the world and others rightly I must first enter into myself. Only once I know what is there, and let chaos become *kosmos*, am I fit to acquire an eye that sees serenely. The wound which a chaste eye inflicts does not humiliate or hurt. It is sweet, like the infant's gaze. It cuts us to the quick but feels like a blessing, reminding us of what sight can be like. To see in this manner is to re-enter paradise, says Bruno. It is part of the process of exchanging the garment of skin for the robe of glory. Sight born of love can become an act of love.

The correlation between seeing and loving is memorably fixed in a gnomic phrase penned by Richard of St Victor, the learned Augustinian born at about the time when Bruno wrote to Raoul and who taught at St Victor in Paris when Eystein Erlendsson, future bishop of Nidaros [Trondheim] and editor of the *Passio Olavi*, was a student there. In his treatise *On Preparing the Soul for Contemplation* he affirmed: '*Ubi amor, ibi oculus.*' That is to say, 'Where there is love, there will be an eye that sees.'

Were I to seek a descriptive term for this kind of seeing, I would call it contemplative. This may surprise. We think of contemplation as a specialized form of prayer reserved for austere professionals. We speak of 'contemplative orders', meaning monastic institutes of enclosure. Contemplation is thought of as a privilege reserved for such environments. Yet the notion points to something pan-human, an exercise without which humanity remains incomplete.

The Renaissance humanists knew this. They stressed it. In Pico della Mirandola's treatise *On the Dignity of Man*, a set text for the generations of the Metaphysical Poets, there is a passage I love very much. Pico describes God's intention in creating human nature. Having made earth and heaven, filling them with life, God longed, says Pico, 'for some creature which might comprehend the meaning of so vast an achievement, which might be moved with love at its beauty and smitten with awe at its grandeur'. Therefore the Almighty set man in the middle of the world as '*universi contemplator*', as someone fit to contemplate the *whole*, sensitive to the connectedness of things and aware of his own rightful place among them.

But what is it really to be a 'contemplator'?

Within 'contemplation' we spot a root familiar from modern vernaculars. It yields words such as 'temple'. Con*templ*ation originates in a cultic setting. We can be more specific, as it happens. The verb *contemplor* first pertained to the vocabulary of bird-flight divination. Imagine an oracle enclosed in a temple looking expectantly out through a hole in the roof, like the one we see in the Roman Pantheon. Patiently, she would look for auspices, omens in the form of avian behaviour by which the gods revealed their good pleasure. Presupposed is the notion that the world is mediatory and significant, pregnant with meaning to be pondered.

Contemplation of this kind was not only practised by solitary augurs cooped up in hallowed houses. It could be a social activity, enabling communities to work out a shared purpose. This is how it is described in the second book of Homer's *Odyssey*, when Telemachus sets out on a quest to seek his missing father. He is concerned about Penelope, his mother, assailed by suitors. He worries about his inheritance. He needs to know whether Odysseus is dead or alive. Before the inhabitants of Ithaca he states his case. The crowd listens keenly. People are sensitive to Telemachus's plight. Mutual attention develops in a horizontal exchange as the

word passes from speaker to assembly, and back. Then
suddenly something happens overhead. Telemachus has
just finished a sentence when:

... τῷ δ᾽ αἰετὼ εὐρύοπα Ζεὺς
ὑψόθεν ἐκ κορυφῆς ὄρεος προέηκε πέτεσθαι.
τὼ δ᾽ ἕως μέν ῥ᾽ ἐπέτοντο μετὰ πνοιῇς ἀνέμοιο
πλησίω ἀλλήλοισι τιταινομένω πτερύγεσσιν·
ἀλλ᾽ ὅτε δὴ μέσσην ἀγορὴν πολύφημον ἱκέσθην,
ἔνθ᾽ ἐπιδινηθέντε τιναξάσθην πτερὰ πυκνά,
ἐς δ᾽ ἰδέτην πάντων κεφαλάς, ὄσσοντο δ᾽ ὄλεθρον·
δρυψαμένω δ᾽ ὀνύχεσσι παρειὰς ἀμφί τε δειρὰς
δεξιὼ ἤιξαν διά τ᾽ οἰκία καὶ πόλιν αὐτῶν.
θάμβησαν δ᾽ ὄρνιθας, ἐπεὶ ἴδον ὀφθαλμοῖσιν·
ὥρμηναν δ᾽ ἀνὰ θυμὸν ἅ περ τελέεσθαι ἔμελλον.

for his sake Zeus of the wide brows sent forth two eagles,
soaring high from the peak of the mountain. These for
a while sailed on the stream of the wind together, wind
and wing, close together, wings spread wide. But when
they were over the middle of the vociferous assembly,
they turned on each other suddenly in a thick shudder
of wings, and swooped over the heads of all, with eyes
glaring and deadly, and tore each other by neck and
cheek with their talons, then sped away to the right
across the houses and city. Then all were astounded at
the birds, when their eyes saw them, and they pondered
in their hearts over what might come of it.

Millennia have passed. Nonetheless this marvellous text still
permits us to sense the excitement of the crowd. All eyes of
a sudden look upward. The assembled mass undulates to the
rhythm of the birds' performance, majestic and menacing.

The spectacle absorbs, yet points beyond itself. The Ithacans know that what they witness *means* something. Something will 'come of it' concerning the matter in hand, namely the possibility of Odysseus's return.

Thus we see what it might mean, in natural terms, to live contemplatively. It is a matter of standing still and watching, paying attention to what happens round about, prepared to step out of our preconceived ideas, alert to the prospect of new-found sense to be weighed in our heart.

This example comes from poetry, but such seeing is no less at the basis of natural science. What does a scientist do, if not observe phenomena of nature in order to establish what they mean? Exclamations of wonder can result, delighted cries of '*Eureka!*'. Some feature in a beautiful book by Richard Dawkins, an anthology of science writing edited as a labour of love. Among the pieces is an excerpt from the astrophysicist Subrahmanyan Chandrasekhar's *Truth and Beauty*, which in turn cites an exchange of two grand physicists, Werner Heisenberg and Albert Einstein. The former shares with the latter this confidence:

> If nature leads us to mathematical forms of great simplicity and beauty – by forms I am referring to coherent systems of hypothesis, axioms, etc. – to forms that no one has previously encountered, we cannot help thinking that they are 'true', that they reveal a genuine feature of nature . . . You must have felt this too: the almost frightening simplicity and wholeness of the relationships which nature suddenly spreads out before us and for which none of us was in the least prepared.

The casual, 'You must have felt this too,' is moving. Dawkins cites Chandrasekhar citing it. This suggests a complicity extending beyond the correspondence of Heisenberg and Einstein, two old friends. Indicated is an aspect of scientific endeavour as such. Heisenberg's association of beauty and truth reaches beyond that of Keats ('Beauty is truth, truth beauty, – that is all/Ye know on earth, and all ye need to know'), which is of the order of sensibility. The beauty in question here is twofold. It is conceptual, apparent in axioms only a trained intelligence can read, but it also unfolds before the eyes, in the 'almost frightening simplicity and wholeness of the relationships which nature suddenly spreads out before us'. The *tremendum* suggests quasi-religious experience. Heisenberg speaks of something revealed. The apocalypse, though, is this-worldly. Nature is the revealing subject. Reverent fear flows from an insight we have pursued from different angles: what is natural is marked by integrity. Nature is essentially chaste.

If this kind of seeing is illumined by faith, a further dimension opens. We find the process described by a contemporary of Heisenberg's, a contemplative in the technical sense: the Carthusian Jean-Baptiste Porion (1899–1987). Porion was a subtle intellectual. At the same time he breathed monastic simplicity. In a letter from 1980 to the philosopher Georges-Hubert de Radkowski, he described contemplative life as '*une découverte inépuisable du même*'. The phrase is hard to render. The 'inexhaustible discovery' regards an object which, in itself, remains the same yet always appears surprising, new. The contemplative gaze, become virginal, is relieved of preconceptions. The beholder is free to encounter the other *as* other, with wonder. Thereby life is released from monotony, infused with freshness.

At stake is not rarified mystical experience, simply a transformed outlook on the world. 'I can't say I've made much of a career in the way of the interior life,' wrote Porion to Charles Journet in 1955, ten years before the latter became a cardinal; 'yet I couldn't conceive the least regret for having set out on it. No, it is a thousand times more interesting to fail in this area than to succeed in any other.'

How this attitude translates into practice is seen in a letter Porion wrote to his sister after a quarter-century of monastic life. We must imagine the setting. A Carthusian lives as a hermit in a little house set on a cloister. The monks gather in church for the long night Vigil, then for Mass and Vespers. The rest of the time is spent, normally, in solitude. When a novice is clothed in the Carthusian habit, the community accompany him to his hermitage, which will be for him a sanctuary. He expects to remain in it until his brothers carry him out into the cemetery. In this life of stability, the window of the monk's cell is a privileged window on the world. Does he not get bored with the view? On the contrary, writes Porion:

> I ascertain the riches contained in a single perspective, the outline of a mountain, say, with its pine trees in the golden glory of May, in the mists of October, or whenever. We must become the mirror of this beauty and its echo. It always reveals something new, yet each time says it all. I do wonder whether travel is worth the bother. What harmony, what inexhaustible harmony, unites the spirit to every being that with divine freedom follows the law imprinted on its nature!

Like the physicist Heisenberg, Porion, the monk, looked out and saw a beautiful wholeness. He was aware of being privy to a kind of revelation. For him, though, the revealing subject was not Mother Nature, but the Creator whose ordering laws nature displays. To learn to see in this way is to discover a significant universe.

This universe beckons to us. It calls forth a response. To sit silently by one's window and look out becomes a *personal* experience: God's sustaining action is present in what exists. 'I make all things new,' says the Lord (Revelation 21.5). This applies even to things that are, in themselves, familiar and old. Porion bears witness that things are *more* than they are in themselves. And that he, contemplating them, becomes more himself when drawn out of himself into a gratuitous encounter.

Chastity enables us to live thus, attentively and reverently. It stands for a way of being alive in the world. It lies within the reach of our choice, though of course we must opt for it reasonably. The liturgy lets us pray for a chaste mind. In a weekday Lauds hymn we find the lines, '*Evincat mentis castitas/quae caro cupit arrogans*': 'May the mind's chastity subdue/what arrogant flesh lusts for.' Chastity relates, here, to meekness, that much under-rated virtue we think of as a dormouse, though it is leonine: courage is called for to combat cupidity's conceit. A chaste mind will inform our interactions. It will shape our actions as well: the way we eat and drink, open and shut doors. We have established the connection between chastity and fasting. Appetites overlap. It is an illusion to think I can be temperate in one without being temperate also in others. Conversely, the clearness of mind and strength of body we find when we fast have equivalents in the realm of chastity.

When Dom Porion looked contemplatively out of his hermitage window, he was alone. But we can see other people, too, in this way, personally. We see them then with *honour*, to pick up a term that in St Benedict's Rule sets the norm for human relationships. To honour someone is to affirm his or her irreducible alterity. It is to recognize their dignity, even when this may be compromised by presumption, fear or base actions. It is to look on them with hope, aware of what they have it in them, by God's grace, to become.

The Gospels give instances of how Christ looked at others. From these we can learn a lot. We have already considered the scene in Simon's house, when he saw the sinful woman approach him yet was not repelled. The fact that he looked at her peacefully transformed her. When, out on a journey, a young man ran up to him and asked how he might know life, 'Jesus, looking at him, loved him,' moved by his sincerity. The youngster was unable to make the decision required to obtain what he longed for. Jesus's gaze left him aggrieved (Mark 10.17-22). Still, for someone to see, without condemning, the conflict of desires that may rage in my heart is benediction. Towards the end of the Gospel, in the high priest's court, he who had been named the Rock denied the One he professed to be Son of God. Jesus, led away to be scourged, 'turned and looked at Peter' (Luke 22.61). The bitterness with which, as a result, Peter wept still rings in our ears thanks to the empathy of Bach's *Passions*.

To be seen in truth is an intimate experience. Sight can in fact be more intimate than touch. As any pastor knows, people often go out in search of sexual adventure because they do not feel seen, suffer from this fact and crave a substitute. The risk is that pleasure serves, then, to exacerbate sadness and make loneliness worse. Intimacy does not have to be sexual. Sex can stand in intimacy's way.

The non-possessive freedom of chaste intimacy shows itself sometimes in shared contemplation of an object exterior to the beholders. Consider these evocative lines in Hans Bethge's rendering of Mong-Kao Jen's poem, 'While Awaiting a Friend', which Gustav Mahler set to music in *Das Lied von der Erde*:

> *Ich sehne mich, o Freund, an deiner Seite*
> *Die Schönheit dieses Abends zu genießen, –*
> *Wo bleibst Du nur? Du läßt mich lang allein!*

> I long, oh my friend, to enjoy
> By your side this evening's loveliness.
> Where are you? You leave me waiting long.

Who has not yearned for someone just to sit like that by our side and be moved by what moves us? When Anton Webern went to hear the first performance of *Das Lied von der Erde* in Munich, this part so moved him that he told Alban Berg he had felt as if his heart rang with the imperative, 'Out with the rubbish! Upwards! *Sursum corda!*' Often our deep desires are purer than we think.

The communion this poem sings of endures. In Jean François Billeter's elegiac homage to his deceased wife Wen, the Swiss Sinologist speaks of the raw grief provoked by the beloved's absence, as if a vital part of himself had been removed. All the more amazing are the sudden moments in which Wen is *there*:

> It suffices to listen to a few bars of music we loved for our *shared* joy to possess me and bowl me over. At such times I need no image of her, no specific remembrance. She is with me in the music.

The tangibly continued reality, beyond separation wrought by death, of shared joy: is that not a validation of chaste love?

At the beginning of the book I cited Norma's question to Clotilde: 'Does your God *heal* hearts sick with love?' We have looked at ways in which healing may happen. The fire of erotic impulse, intrinsic to human nature, can brighten and warm our lives as a source of gladness and fruitfulness. It can also erupt in conflagrations of deadly passion. In a Christian optic, *eros* is an impulse towards the divine, but it is not itself divine. It has its part to play in ordering human existence towards its true goal, the knowledge and love of God. It must not be mistaken for the goal.

The Church refuses to either absolutize or materialize *eros* and, in consequence, sexuality. That is, here and now, a counter-cultural position to assume, but the here and now will pass. The Christian vision of human nature endures.

While the Church regards kindly those who struggle to live by the commandments, she insists that with God's help it is possible; not only can it be done, it can make us flourish. 'Choose life!' (Deuteronomy 30.19). This imperative holds. A Christian desires and is called to be fully alive, no less. But sometimes we need help to know what life is and where it is found. We need to be taught where we come from, where we are going, what means we have at our disposal, who is there to help us. This book is a modest attempt to provide a few indications.

'Be reconciled to God', writes Paul to the Corinthians (2 Corinthians 5.20). The injunction regards our passage from enmity to friendship with God. It can also be read existentially, as if to say, 'Be unto God people who are reconciled.' Herein lies a call to integrity and self-acceptance, to live with our longings, limitations and losses. We must accept the fact of being persons, turned towards and needing others, not self-sufficient individuals. We must accept our need to be saved: the disorder we carry is more than we can sort out on our own. Like musical instruments, we must be harmonized, rightly attuned by a pitch not of this world. The reconciliation of the senses is part of this enterprise. Chastity equilibrates it. It points, not to mindless mortification, but rather, as Pavel Florensky wrote in an exuberant text, 'to wholeness, healthiness, unimpairedness, unity of the inner life, in general to the normal state of the inner life, to a person's unfragmentedness and strength, to freshness of spiritual powers, to the spiritual organizedness of the inner man'.

Antiquity's emblem of chastity, Diana, was lovely but fierce. She had several strings to her bow. She was goddess, too, of the hunt and of fertility: ancient idols commonly show her many-breasted. The early preachers of the Gospel clashed with her adherents at Ephesus. Christianity's progress had occasioned a decline in the trade of local silversmiths who made little shrines to Diana. A trade-union riot resulted, described in the Acts of the Apostles (19.23ff.). People cheered for Diana at the top of their voices, causing commotion, threatening violence. Ephesus was a town in which attitudes to the body could issue in militancy.

To the Ephesians Paul traced the outline of what, much later, would be called a theology of the body: 'no one ever hates his own body, but he nourishes and tenderly cares for it, just as Christ does for the church' (Ephesians 5.29). Neither fertility nor chastity, Paul suggests, can be reduced to ideological positioning. Only a mystagogical, sacramental perspective will do them justice.

Diana was jealous of her purity. Ovid tells of Actaeon happening upon her one day while she was bathing in a grove. Diana was furious. She glared at him, 'blushed like a dawn cloud', reached for her arrows. Finding none, she splashed him with water and shouted, 'Now, if you can, tell how you saw me naked.' No sooner had she spoken than Actaeon was subject to troubling metamorphosis. Antlers burst from his forehead, 'his ears/Folded to whiskery points, his hands were hooves,/His arms long slender legs.' Terror filled his heart. He had become a deer. The fact of having drawn too close to naked virtue had made of him an animal.

The Christian embodiment of chastity would assume a different character. The early Church saw it above all in the Virgin Martyrs, those young heroines (Agatha, Lucy, Agnes and Cecilia) whose names we still repeat daily in the Roman Canon of the Mass. Chastity, we have seen, is not coterminous with celibacy. But sexual continence practised in the name of faith bears privileged witness to chastity. The Virgin Martyrs show that the following of Christ is worthy of such sacrifice; further, that one may, nurtured by friendship and sacramental grace, forego an active sexual life and yet be joyful and fulfilled, maturing to full stature, transmitting life.

Cecilia was a Roman maiden engaged to a youth named Valerian during the papacy of Urban I (222–30). Graced illumination gave her knowledge of what Paul expounded to the Church at Ephesus as a mystery of faith. She was given certainty that Christ was the spouse of her soul and that this nuptial compact would define her in time and for eternity. She prayed that Valerian might come to understand what this meant. Her prayer was heard. The two resolved to live together in virginity. This was not because they were frightened of sex or thought sex unclean. It was because they had glimpsed the state of union with God which human sexuality exists to signify. In the normal run of things, spousal intimacy will direct bodies and minds towards this union. In the case of Cecilia and Valerian the process worked the other way round: union with God revealed the sense of earthly nuptials.

Cecilia's Christian witness caused scandal in a city still largely pagan. She was arrested, then condemned to suffocation in the baths. When the city's prefect heard she was still alive after 24 hours, he ordered decapitation. The henchman struck thrice, unable to sever the head from the trunk. Roman law did not permit a fourth attempt. He left Cecilia bleeding, therefore. She lived on for three days. Then she died, and was buried by Pope Urban. This story, told in ancient chronicles, was confirmed by observation in the jubilee year of 1600. During restoration works at the abbey of Santa Cecilia in Trastevere, on the site where Cecilia's family had held its *titulus*, the martyr's remains were found. Not only were they, like those of the Carthusian dug up at Miraflores, in a state of incorruption. The twisted position of Cecilia's head also corresponded exactly to the story of failed execution. The find was a sensation. Swiss guards had to be brought in to control the traffic of pilgrims wanting to pray in the physical presence of one of Rome's most beloved saints.

Among them was the sculptor Stefano Maderno. He saw the body, and rendered what he saw in marble. His monument – unforgettable – is displayed to this day underneath the abbey church's main altar. One day in mid-November 1887, the fourteen-year-old Thérèse Martin from Lisieux knelt before it. She had travelled to Rome to ask the Pope to let her enter Carmel despite her young age. St Cecilia had until that day meant little to her. She had known her as patron saint of music, assuming Cecilia had acquired this role because she sang well. In Rome she found that, no, the reason was another: the proclamation had been made 'in remembrance of the virginal song of praise she sang to her Divine Spouse hidden in her heart of hearts'. At once Thérèse felt for her 'the tenderness of a friend'. The harmony of Cecilia's life was what she wished for. A compelling example of generative chastity was present to her, in that venerable church, in the form of an inward song.

Maderno's statue underneath the high altar in the Basilica of Santa Cecilia in Trastevere, in a drawing by J. Petot that featured in the geographical journal *Il Giro del mondo* on 9 June 1870. How remarkable to produce such a lifelike image of one dead.

Thérèse did not have the option of ascending to the gallery of the abbey church to see a work of art that takes the modern visitor's breath away. Pietro Cavallini's west wall fresco of the Last Judgement, painted around 1300, was hidden by a secondary wall during redesign in the 1720s, another example of how fashions change. Only in 1900 was it recovered. Today it is considered the first example of modern painting in Rome, antedating Giotto's work at the Lateran. At the centre is Christ, the universal Judge, bearing the wounds of the Passion, robed in imperial purple. Worshippers pass under him as they leave the church, reminded that to be human is to be answerable. 'Adam, where are you?' A response is called for. Accountability pertains to our dignity. Responsibility for our choices is part of the texture of our glorious robe. Christ's outstretched right hand does not dismiss or repel. It signals elevation. It shows the height to which we must aspire, which he would help us reach.

Flanking Christ are gorgeously coloured angels with wings so vivid one can hear them flutter. As they ascend, they become increasingly incorporeal, assumed into sublimity. The angels make me think of something Menuhin once said about the Adagio movement of Beethoven's Violin Sonata No. 10 in G Major: 'Those opening twelve bars – the wonderful sense of rhythmic continuity and this extraordinary serenity of Beethoven. It's a kind of shedding of everything that is flesh. And yet it remains human.' Needless to say, a man is not an angel. The Word's incarnation bestowed on human nature a distinction surpassing that of cherubim and seraphim. Nonetheless Cavallini's angels convey a message to us. They recall St Paul's assurance: 'We shall not all sleep, but we shall all be changed, in a moment, in the twinkling of an eye' (1 Corinthians 15.51f.). We cannot imagine what this change will be like; how the integrity of our iconic nature will manifest itself in an eternal reality unnarrowed by space and time; but we should think about it, often. 'For now we see in a mirror dimly, but then face to face' (1 Corinthians 13.12).

On either side of the angels the apostles are enthroned, six to the right, six to the left. Their features are vivid, a world apart from the stylized depictions of the ninth-century mosaic in the apse at the church's opposite end. For this book's front cover, I have chosen the portrait of Matthew, a man transformed by meeting Christ's gaze. The Lord found him in a place of shame, but was not ashamed to call him; no, he accompanied him home, into the life this average man had built for himself in the lowlands, not yet knowing what heights existence may reach. Jesus subverted this familiar world, not obliterating it, but showing its insufficiency to fulfil the supernatural desire that lay dormant in coin-counting Matthew. The presence of God's Son had awakened it. The tax collector could not, thenceforth, keep walking about in garments of skin. He longed to be reclothed with the robe of glory.

From the outset, Matthew observed Jesus closely. That is plain from the Gospel he wrote, rich in detail. St Dominic, that most humane of preachers, carried the Gospel of Matthew on his person at all times, we are told. It was for him an invaluable resource as he preached to the Cathars, rationalists who struggled to accept the theological significance of ordinary life and of the human body.

According to the *Legenda Aurea*, Matthew brought the Gospel to Scythia after the Lord's resurrection. People there did not like their established notions to be challenged in Christ's name. To keep themselves out of the preacher's sight, they blinded him. By a miracle,

Matthew's vision was restored. Decades earlier the light of glory had touched him while he sat immersed in the murk of his customs booth. He was someone who had known both metaphorically and physically the interchange of darkness and light. He had learned not to fear it. That is why he could teach others with authority not to be afraid.

Cavallini represents Matthew as a young man. He upholds the cross with resolve, yet his face is marked by an expression of inquisitive kindness. His eyes look towards the glorified Son of God, whom the Church invokes as the Desired of the Nations. In him God satisfies our deep aspirations with good things, restoring the iconic potential of our nature. We hope at the last, at the opportune time, to stand before his throne integral and free. Then he will crown our everlasting youth, restored like an eagle's, with joy (cf. Psalms 102.5, 42.4).

Meanwhile we progress with patience from what is partial to what is whole, ordering and making chaste our bodies, souls and minds in the obedience of charity. The eyes of our love are opened thereby. We pass from blindness to sight. The journey is laborious at times, but leads through lovely landscapes. The further we travel, the more keenly we are conscious that we do not walk alone.

Notes

Except when noted, translations are mine. Scripture is normally cited from the *RSV*.

Norma's Question

It is in Shakespeare's *Othello* III.3 that the Moor says of Desdemona, 'Her name, that was as fresh as Dian's visage, is now begrimed and black as my own face.' Cicero explains Diana's epithet '*omnivaga*' in *De natura deorum* II.68. He adds, beautifully, '*Diana dicta quia noctu quasi diem efficeret*': 'She was called Diana because, in the night, she brought about a kind of day.' Aristotle explains the meaning of 'catharsis' in the sixth part of his *Poetics*. To illustrate Cicero's uses of '*castus*' I cite from his *De divinatione*, I.53, and from the first *Tusculan Disputation* (*De contemnenda morte*), I.30. Gellius's remark on Caesar's style is taken from *Nox Philologiae: Aulus Gellius and the Fantasy of the Roman Library* 'by Anonymous, edited and with an introduction by Erik Gunderson' (Madison, Wisconsin: University of Wisconsin Press, 2009), p. 88, citing the *Noctes Atticae*, 19.8.3. A potted biography of German '*Keuschheit*' is available in that marvellous resource, *Digitales Wörterbuch der deutschen Sprache*. Roger Nichols gives the account of Poulenc's night at the opera in *Poulenc: A Biography* (New Haven and London: Yale University Press, 2020), p. 254. That particular evening, Callas had sung Verdi, but her comportment was characteristic. Poulenc's companion Hervé Dugardin said, 'You should write an opera just for her . . . that way she wouldn't be such a b— nuisance.' This inspired Poulenc's *La Voix humaine* for a single soprano. The sources of *Norma* are examined by Damien Colas in 'Aux sources du personnage de Norma', *Bollettino di Studi Belliniani* 1 (2015), 5–36. The exchange between Norma and Clotilde in Soumet's play (Paris: Barba, 1831) takes place in Scene

Four of Act One. Romani's libretto to Bellini's opera is readily available online. I have cited the Greek text of Cavafy's *Ithaca* from Constantine A. Trypanis's *The Penguin Book of Greek Verse* (London: Penguin, 1971), p. 585f. The translation is Peter Bien's, taken from his *Greek Today: A Course in the Modern Language and Culture* (Hanover and London: University Press of New England, 2004), p. xxxvii.

What a Human Being *Is*

The substance of the offertory prayer, *Deus qui humanitatis*, is found in the sixth-century *Sacramentarium Leonianum*. The first part, '*Deus qui humanae substantiae dignitatem mirabiliter condidisti et mirabilius reformasti*', has inexplicably dropped out of the present form of the Roman-rite Mass, but is maintained in the collect for Christmas Day. The intrinsic connection between Genesis 1.27 and Colossians 1.13-15 is drawn already in Origen's first homily on Genesis. A critical edition of *The Cave of Treasures* is available in Syriac with an accompanying French translation in the *Corpus Scriptorum Christianorum Orientalium*: *La Caverne des trésors: Les deux recensions syriaques*, ed. Su-Min Ri, *CSCO*, 486–7, Scriptores syri, 207–8 (Louvain: Peeters, 1987). For the sake of clarity, I have sometimes abbreviated passages cited from this work. The article by Su-Min Ri referred to is 'La Caverne des Trésors et Mar Éphrem', in *Orientalia Christiana Analecta* 256 (1998), p. 82f. I have cited E.A. Wallis Budge from the preface to his translation of *The Cave of Treasures*, based on an edition now viewed as unreliable, published in London by the Religious Tracts Society in 1927. This can be found online at www.sacred-texts .com/chr/bct/. The Arabic version was edited and translated into Italian by Bellarmino Bagatti and Antonio Battista (Jerusalem: Franciscan Printing Press, 1979). The baptismal prayer is part of '*Ordines baptismi & confirmationis Jacobi Edesseni*', in H. Denzinger, *Ritus orientalium*, I (Würzburg, 1863), p. 288. Precious resources for general background to this tradition of exegesis are Michael E. Stone's *A History of the Literature of Adam and Eve* (Atlanta: Scholars Press, 1992) and Sebastian Brock's *The Luminous Eye: The Spiritual World Vision of Saint Ephrem the*

Syrian (Kalamazoo: Liturgical Press (Cistercian Publications), 1992). The passage from the Lament of Adam is from Sophrony Sakharov, *Saint Silouan the Athonite*, trans. Rosemary Edmonds (Tolleshunt Knights: Monastery of St John the Baptist, 1991), p. 451. Thomas Merton's statement about St Silouan – 'the most authentic monk' – is widely cited but difficult to track down. Dr Paul Pearson of the Thomas Merton Center finally traced it for me to the French edition of *Monastic Peace*, published as *La Paix monastique* in 1961 by Albin Michel. The phrase does not appear in the English version, so Merton must have added it to the materials he sent his French translator, Marie Tadié.

Tensions

The title of Panayotis Nellas in the original is a splendid phrase borrowed from Gregory Nazianzen: *Zōon theoumenon*, meaning, 'a living creature that is being deified'. Norman Russell's fine translation compacts this into *Deification in Christ* (Crestwood, New York: St Vladimir's Seminary Press, 1997).

Body and Soul

The story of Olav's proto-miracle is from the second chapter of the *Passio Olavi*. The account of how his hair and nails kept growing is told in *Heimskringla*, in the 'Saga of St Olav', par. 245. E. Allison Peers's tribute to his Carthusian friend constitutes an appendix to *Saint Teresa of Jesus and other Essays and Addresses* (London: Faber and Faber, 1953). I have drawn my quotations from Hesse's *Siddhartha* from the first two chapters of Part Two. The quotation from Tim Winton's *Breath* (London: Picador, 2008) occurs on p. 23. *Danseuse classique* is cited from Emil Boyson, *Utvalgte dikt* (Oslo: Gyldendal, 1959). Virginia Woolf's caustic remark about Lydia Lopokova, Mrs John Maynard Keynes, was cited in Judith Flanders' review of Judith Mackrell's *Bloomsbury Ballerinas* in the *TLS* on 20 June 2008.

Male and Female

Buber's translation of the Hebrew Bible, a work he began in tandem with Franz Rosenzweig, then finished alone, is a marvel. It has done more than any other text to open up the Old Testament to me. It is available as *Die Schrift* in a remarkably cheap edition published by the Deutsche Bibelgesellschaft. For Rashi's Commentary on Genesis I use Luigi Cattani's Italian translation published by Marietti in 2011. Not many people read the exegetical work of Paul Claudel. A pity. It has been brought together in two large volumes entitled *Le Poëte et la Bible*, edited by M. Malicet, X. Tilliette and D. Millet-Gérard (Paris: Gallimard, 1998 and 2004). The passages cited in this chapter, though, are from chapter 4 of a work more general in scope: *Seigneur, apprenez-nous à prier* (Paris: Gallimard, 1942). It was translated by Ruth Bethell and published as *Lord, Teach Us to Pray* in New York by Longmans and Green in 1948. I have cited Jacques Lusseyran from the second edition of his *Conversation amoureuse: De l'amour à l'Amour*, published in Paris by Éditions Triades in 2005. I propose my reading of תְּשׁוּקָה notwithstanding the learned theses put forward by my teacher and friend A. A. Macintosh in 'The Meaning of Hebrew תְּשׁוּקָה', published in the *Journal of Semitic Studies* LXI/2 (2016), 365–87, a paper that argues for a less pugnacious definition. It is in the documentary *Tystnad, Tagning, Trollflöjten* from 1975 that Ingmar Bergman likens Mozart's opera to a gospel.

Order and Disorder

Ephrem's description of Adam's priestly service comes from the *Hymns on Paradise* 3.16, translated by Sebastian Brock (Crestwood, New York: St Vladimir's Seminary Press, 1990). The theme of the ordering of love is developed in St Bernard's sermons 49–51 on the Song of Songs. The programme *Yehudi Menuhin, The Violin of the Century* was produced in 1994 by Ideale Audience/La Sept – Arte Imalyre. I have cited Etty Hillesum's *An Interrupted Life and Letters from Westerbork* in Arnold J. Pomerans' translation first published in 1983 (New York: Holt, 1996). The quotation from Lusseyran's *Et la lumière fut* (Paris: Le Félin, 2008) is taken from the end of chapter 10 of Part Two.

Eros and Death

I cite Athanasius's text in R.C. Gregg's version, contained in *The Life of Antony and the Letter to Marcellinus* (New York, Ramsey,

Toronto: Paulist Press, 1980). The Davidization of the Psalter is treated in greater depth in my essay, 'Cum Davide versari: The Psalter as Acquired Self-Expression', in A Book of Psalms from Eleventh-Century Byzantium: The Complex of Texts and Images in Vat. Gr. 752, edited by Barbara Crostini and Glenn Peters (Vatican: Biblioteca Apostolica Vaticana, Studi e testi 504, 2016). St Benedict's instruction regarding Psalm 50 is found in chapter 13 of the Holy Rule. Wyatt's version of Psalm 50 is cited from Sir Thomas Wyatt, The Complete Poems, edited by R.A. Rebholz (London: Penguin, 2015). The passages defining 'eros' are, of course, from Pope Benedict XVI's encyclical, Deus caritas est, n. 4. Christoph Schlingensief writes of the music of Wagner in the entry marked 10 February in So schön wie hier kanns im Himmel gar nicht sein! Tagebuch einer Krebserkrankung (Cologne: Kiepenheuer & Witsch, 2009). Gwen Ffrangcon-Davies spoke of Flagstad to Sue Lawley on Desert Island Discs on 19 June 1988. Harold Pinter's Ashes to Ashes was published by Faber and Faber in London in 1996. Gitta Sereny speaks of the play in The German Trauma: Experiences and Reflections 1938–2000 (London: Allen Lane, 2000), p. 286f. Pinter's remark about its background is cited in a book he sent Sereny for reference: Michael Billington's The Life and Work of Harold Pinter (London: Faber and Faber, 1996), p. 374f. Vincent Canby's review of The Night Porter was printed in the New York Times on 13 October 1974. Liliana Cavani explains the background of the film in the retrospective 'Liliana Cavani on The Night Porter' directed by David Gregory in 2006. The testimony of the former nun, a victim of abuse, is drawn from Dom Dysmas de Lassus's important book, Risques et dérives de la vie religieuse (Paris: Cerf, 2020), p. 429ff. Somaly Mam's memoir, first out in French, was published in Lisa Appignanesi's translation as The Road of Lost Innocence (London: Virago, 2007.) Quotations are from pp. 35, 38, 51, 58, 62 and 101. Anyone tempted to think Mam's extreme experience categorically distinct from that of glamorous, well-paid, developed-world pornographic actors might consider the story told in Tomer Heymann's 2018 documentary, Jonathan Agassi Saved My Life. Jennifer Lash (alias Jini Fiennes) died in 1993, at 55. Blood Ties was published posthumously (London: Bloomsbury, 1997). Quotations are from pp. 239, 242, 244f., 276ff.

Marriage and Virginity

Shlomo Alkabets's hymn לְכָה דוֹדִי and Rabbi Sacks's notes can be found in *The Authorised Daily Prayer Book of the United Hebrew Congregations of the Commonwealth,* 4th edition, with new translation and commentary by Chief Rabbi Sir Jonathan Sacks (London: Collins, 2007), pp. 255, 266-69. R.A. Markus cites Paphnutius and has many other interesting things to say about marriage and sexuality in the early Church in *The End of Ancient Christianity* (Cambridge: Cambridge University Press, 1990), p. 38. The quotation from Ida Görres occurs on p. 20 of her essay, *Von Ehe und von Einsamkeit* (Stuttgart-Degerloch: Auer, 1949). The quotations from Marilynne Robinson's *Jack* (London: Virago, 2020), are on pp. 208 and 163. I have cited the Rite of Consecration of Virgins according to the *Monastic Ritual* approved for the use of the Abbey of Sainte Cécile de Solesmes in 1975, kindly placed at my disposal by the nuns of St Cecilia's Abbey, Ryde. On Thursday of the 2nd week of Lent, the Church recites the prayer beginning, '*Deus, innocentiae restitutor et amator*'. The passages cited from George Mackay Brown's *Magnus* (London: The Hogarth Press, 1973), are taken from the first few pages of Part 4, 'The Temptations'. The account of how the book was written is recorded in chapter 15 of Maggie Fergusson's *George Mackay Brown: The Life* (London: John Murray, 2006). Pope Francis's Apostolic Letter *Patris Corde*, on St Joseph, was published on 8 December 2020. I have cited from chapter 7, 'A Father in the Shadows'. In this same sense St Benedict tells the abbot, in chapter 64 of the Holy Rule, to be chaste. He is to pour out his life for the sons whom providence entrusts to his care, but not for a moment is he to think that they belong to him.

Freedom and Ascesis

The passage from Nicholas Kavasilas's *The Life in Christ* (PG 150, 680A) is cited in Nellas's *Deification in Christ*, p.223. The saying, 'Look up, not down' features in an *apophthegm* (XVIII.13) attributed to Abba Macarius. John XXIII's encyclical *Mater et Magistra* on Christianity and social progress was published on 15 May 1961. Irenaeus's text about Adam's childishness is from chapter 12 of *The Apostolic Preaching*.

The phrase from the *Epistle to Diognetus* occurs in that text's chapter 9. Jean Cardinal Daniélou died on 20 May 1974. Gunnel Vallquist published *Följeslagare* some months later (Stockholm: Bonnier, 1975). The statement to which I refer occurs towards the end of her chapter on Daniélou. Athanasius speaks of believers' commitment to virginity in chapter 51 of *De incarnatione*. *Urett – et essay om overgrep, en opera og teoriene fra Paris* (Oslo: Humanist Forlag, 2022) by Martin Wåhlberg, Professor of Literature at Trondheim, and examines attitudes tending to justify paedophilia in Foucault, Matzneff and other luminaries of the French literary pantheon. Of course, we find similar tendencies in other contexts and countries, too, astonished that they were ever propagated. I have cited Yourcenar's remarks on sublimation in Dori Katz's translation, prepared in collaboration with the author. The passage occurs at the end of the introduction to *Fires* (New York: Farrar, Straus and Giroux, 1981). The Norwegian primary school manual *Solaris 3–4*, written by Astrid Munkebye, Eli Munkebye and Kristin Skage, was published in Oslo by Aschehough in 2022. The twin counsels about loving chastity and fasting are given in chapter 4 of St Benedict's Rule. I have cited John Climacus from the fifth chapter, 'On Penitence', of *The Ladder of Divine Ascent* in the superb translation of Colm Luibheid and Norman Russell (New York: Paulist Press, 1982), p. 129. Rainer Maria Rilke's *Briefe an einen jungen Dichter* were published in Leipzig by Insel-Verlag in 1929. The translation is Reginald Snell's (London: Sidgwick and Jackson, 1945) – what a marvellous text to divulge right after the war. Athanasius describes Antony as being 'ὡς ὑπὸ τοῦ λόγου κυβερνώμενος', 'like someone governed by the Logos', when he emerged from the fortress in the desert after many years' seclusion, surprising everyone by being 'fully equal to himself', i.e. in perfect balance (*Vita Antonii*, 14).

NEGOTIATING PASSION

Knut Hamsun wrote *Victoria* in 1898. It is available in several English translations. On the interplay between Athanasius's *Life of Antony* and his *De incarnatione*, see Louis Bouyer's *La Vie de*

S. Antoine: Essai sur la spiritualité du monachisme primitif, 2nd edition (Bellefontaine: Éditions de Bellefontaine, 1977). His statement on the eschatological significance of celibacy is from *De incarnatione* 51.1. The story of Antony's vocation is told in chapter 2 of the *Vita Antonii*; his deathbed confession is related in chapter 91. Quotations from the *Apophthegmata* are referenced in the text on the basis of the three-volume 'systematic' edition published in *Sources Chrétiennes.* Nellas speaks of the monk retracing Adam's path in reverse in *Deification,* p. 90. A seminal study of monastic repentance remains Irénée Hausherr's *Penthos: The Doctrine of Compunction in the Christian East,* translated into English by Anselm Hufstader (Collegeville: Liturgical Press, 1982). Nikolai Leskov develops the *topos* of monks' encountering worldly examples of virtue in his charming story *Pamfalon the Clown.*

CONTEMPLATIVE LIFE

The passage cited from St Bruno's letter to his friend Raoul, written in the 90s of the eleventh century, is from par. 6. The text can be found in many languages on the Carthusians' website, www.chartreux.org. Gregory's description of St Benedict's solitude is from the Second Book of the *Dialogues,* chapter 5. Richard of St Victor's *Ubi amor, ibi oculus* features in his treatise *On Preparing the Soul for Contemplation,* or *Benjamin Minor,* par. 13. It is still most conveniently found in Migne's *Patrologia Latina* 196, c. 10. A nice edition of Pico della Mirandola's *De hominis dignitate* is published by the Scuola superiore normale di Pisa (Pisa: Edizioni della Normale, 2012). A. Robert Caponigri's English version (Chicago: Gateway, 1956) is available on the internet. In the pagination of reference, the passage cited can be found at 131r. I have cited Richard Lattimore's translation of *The Odyssey,* II., 146–57 (London: HarperCollins, 2007). Heisenberg's remark to Einstein is found in *The Oxford Book of Modern Science Writing,* edited by Richard Dawkins (Oxford: Oxford University Press, 2008), p. 350. Keats's line on truth and beauty concludes his *Ode on a Grecian Urn.* The quotations from Dom Jean-Baptiste Porion, *Lettres et écrits spirituels* (Paris: Beauchesne, 2012), edited by Nathalie Nabert, can be found on pp. 123, 38, 26. This book is a treasure. In the fourth chapter of the Holy Rule, St Benedict counsels, '*Honorare omnes homines*'. A look at a concordance of the Rule will reveal the importance of this term in his vocabulary. The theme of Jesus's transformative way of seeing others is developed in a valuable essay by Luigi d'Ayala Valva, *Lo sguardo di Gesù* (Bose: Qiqajon, 2016). Bethge's text and Webern's letter to Berg are cited in Eberhard G. Bethge's *Hans Bethge: Leben und Werk* (Kelkheim: YinYang, 2002), pp. 31 and 37. Jean François Billeter's *Une autre Aurélia* was published in Paris by Allia in 2017. The quotation is from p. 27. A powerful testimony! Pavel Florensky's *The Pillar and Ground of the Truth: An Essay in Orthodox Theodicy in Twelve Letters* has been translated into English by Boris Jakim (Princeton: Princeton University Press, 2004). The passage on chastity is found in the seventh letter. Actaeon's encounter with Diana is retold in Ted Hughes's *Tales from Ovid* (London: Faber and Faber, 1997), ever a source of delight, from which I have drawn my quotations. Thérèse of Lisieux reappraises St Cecilia on page A 61 *verso* of *Histoire d'une âme*. Again, I have drawn Yehudi Menuhin's wisdom from the interview with Bruno Monsaingeon, referenced above. The anecdote about St Dominic carrying Matthew's Gospel is from the *Acta canonizationis* cited in the breviary for Vigils on his feast day, 8 August. James of Voragine recounts the legend of Matthew's blinding and healing in his chapter on St Andrew. The Church calls on Christ as '*Desideratus gentium*' in the O Antiphon for vespers three days before Christmas, on 22 December. On that day the collect reads as follows: 'God and Father, you looked in pity on fallen man and redeemed us by the coming of your Son. Grant that we who profess our firm and humble faith in the incarnation of our Redeemer may have a share in his divine life.'

As *Chastity* was going to press I was alerted to the controversy surrounding the memoirs of Somaly Mam, accused of making up parts of her story. I cannot answer for its integrity in every detail; but have chosen to keep the passages cited, which give voice to generic experience. Whether Mam has drawn on her or others' history, the account is corroborated by like testimonies. It goes to show how careful one must be with regard to one's sources, even prize-winning ones.